THE SUNDAY TIMES
Gardener's Almanac

THE SUNDAY TIMES
Gardener's Almanac

GRAHAM ROSE

Roger Houghton
London

First published 1986
Text © Times Newspapers Ltd and Graham Rose 1985, 1986
Illustrations © Times Newspapers Ltd 1985, 1986
Diagrams by John Grimwade © Times Newspapers Ltd 1985, 1986

Set in Linotron Garamond by
Gee Graphics Limited, London
Printed and bound in Spain by Graficromo, S.A., Córdoba
for Roger Houghton Ltd, in association with J M Dent
and Sons Limited, Aldine House,
33 Welbeck Street, London WIM 8LX

Illustrations on pages 13, 53, 91 by Shirley Felts;
on pages 23, 63, 101, by Rosanne Sanders;
on pages 43, 83, 117 by Jenny Tylden-Wright;
on pages 33, 73, 109 by Nicki Kemball.
All other illustrations by Angela Barrett.

British Library Cataloguing in Publication Data

Rose, Graham
    The Sunday Times gardener's almanac.
    1. Gardening
    I. Title
    635   SB450.97

    ISBN 1 85203 009 7

Contents

AUTHOR'S ACKNOWLEDGEMENT

Special thanks are due to my colleagues on the *The Sunday Times Colour Magazine* and the illustrators, who did so much to make the almanacs on which this book is based such a popular feature.

Foreword

There is no better way of organising a work schedule than by making a list of jobs and ticking them off one by one. It is easy enough when you're planning a dinner party or packing for a holiday, but in the garden, where so many things happen simultaneously, it will work only if you devote a great deal of time and thought to the creation of your list. Every task has its time, and if you miss it you can too easily lose a season's colour or spoil a crop.

Although particular operations are scheduled to be carried out at specific times in this book, the almanac can only act as a general guide. Garden operations should be determined by local conditions as much as the calendar. So in more northerly places or late seasons some tasks might have to be delayed by up to three weeks, and in favoured corners of the south or unusually warm seasons the date of operations will need to be advanced.

The 'Plant of the Month' lists relate to plants which are at their best in that particular month; any garden containing some from each selection should have something pleasant to show at all seasons.

January

A good housekeeping month – January is a time for maintenance, repairs, preparation. Thoughtful, steady work now is the way to avoid summertime chaos and the best guarantee of heavy crops and beds full of blooms. Don't be put off by the weather: sharp winter days spent among the frosted plants and glistening berries can be positively therapeutic, especially after all that Christmas torpor.

Ground work

Whenever the ground is dry, try to complete any deep digging. Prepare the soil for vegetables and, if you want to make major changes in the shape of beds by digging up lawns etc., now is the time. Leave the surface soil loose and rough to obtain the maximum benefit from weathering in the weeks to come. If you are working on new paths, terraces or steps, remember to protect the lawn from barrow wheel marks with a stout plank.

Fork a light dressing of manure or compost into the areas of flower beds where you plan to establish bedding plants this summer. Fork over the beds between clumps of perennial plants, burying weed seedlings and digging out deep-rooted perennial weeds. Dead-head and cut back the remains of late blooms as you work past them. Sweet pea land which has previously been double-dug and has had as much organic manure as possible incorporated with the bottom split of soil should now be sweetened by scattering ½lb per square yard of hydrated lime.

In the vegetable patch, break up the soil surface between growing crops by light hoeing. Clear away unwanted remains of crops and use them to start your new compost heap.

Pruning

Finish pruning apples, pears and plums. Cut back and trim beech, hawthorn or privet hedges and prune all the other deciduous shrubs. Cut back the stems of newly planted blackberries, raspberries, loganberries, tayberries, boysenberries etc. to within 1ft of the soil. Halve the lead shoots of gooseberry and red and white currant bushes. Cut blackcurrants well back and keep strong, unblemished shoots to use as cuttings.

Security

Make sure all important stems of wall plants are firmly tied to supports. Go round autumn-planted trees, shrubs and roses, firming them in with the foot if they have been loosened by wind or frost. Make sure that ties to stakes are tight. Protect fruit trees from future pests and disease by spraying them with a tar oil wash which will also clean up the bark. Wrap up dwarf rhododendrons and Japanese azaleas in transparent polythene sheet on nights when frost is imminent. Remove the sheet during the day. Check stored fruit and discard anything showing rot before it infects the entire crop.

Protect rhubarb crowns from frost with a thick layer of straw. (A patch of carpet underfelt or glassfibre roof insulation works equally well.) Keep autumn-sown annuals under light cloches or sheets of transparent polythene supported by sticks. Even a lump of wood on either side of the rows will offer useful protection from the worst of the wind and frost.

Cleaning and tidying

Examine all woodwork in the garden and greenhouse. Cut out and replace any rotted timber, then treat everything with a preservative fluid. Spray stone and brick paths and terraces with an algicide to prevent them becoming slippery. Sweep dead leaves and rubbish from paths and terraces and treat them with total weedkiller on a calm day.

Drag all dead leaves and broken twigs from under hedges. Burn the twigs and create a separate compost heap for the leaves – don't mix them with ordinary compost because they break down too slowly. Tidy the centres of clumps of pinks, removing dead or weakly stems.

Take everything which doesn't need protection out of the potting shed and greenhouse. Throw plant and soil remains on to the compost heap and then scrub out all the pots and seed boxes with Jeyes fluid, rinse them well and leave them stacked for use later. Give the shed and house a thorough brush-out and wash with disinfectant.

Outdoor planting

Plant new trees, shrubs and rhubarb crowns on days when frost is not imminent. Begin propagation of shrubs with thin low branches by 'layering': peg a section of the branch into a clay pot of compost set right into the soil. Save money in future by taking cuttings of ripe young stems of deciduous trees and shrubs and planting them in a well-drained trench in which the soil has been mixed with peat and sand. New blackcurrant bushes can also be produced in this way from cuttings obtained during pruning.

Transplant well-rooted suckers detached from roses grown on their own stock, lilacs and other shrubs. Plant lily bulbs in well-drained soil; choose the short varieties which won't need staking.

New herb gardens in sunny situations can be planted by the end of the month and you can also plant rows of shallots

(barely cover their tops) in a well-drained corner of the vegetable plot.

Outdoor sowing

Sow a few lettuce and radish every fortnight from the middle of the month, and broad beans and peas at the end of the month.

Feeding

Spread 1oz per square yard of hoof and horn meal over peach and nectarine roots. Apply nitrogen fertiliser to trees in grassed orchards.

Lawn work

Land to be sown with lawnseed in March should be thoroughly dug and allowed to stand rough to weather. On a very dry day give the lawn its winter mowing with

Clematis cirrhosa. Plant it on a frost-free day against one of your warmer walls and by this time next year you'll have a magnificent covering of evergreen foliage and lovely bell-shaped flowers which will last through until the following March

the blades set high; this helps break up the residue of tree leaves, making them easier for worms to bury. Turf can be laid to renew worn areas or establish new lawn. When the grass is dry aerate the damper areas; deep pricking with a fork or an aerator will improve drainage.

Maintenance

After the winter tidying get the lawn mower overhauled and ground and reset along with saws and clippers. Examine and replace defective handles on tools such as 10lb hammers, picks, mattocks, rakes, hoes, spades and forks. Overhaul the motor cultivator and any other mechanical implements.

In the greenhouse

Sow lily seed in boxes and bring in pot lilies for forcing. Sow onions, globe beetroot, stump-rooted carrots, leeks, early peas and radishes in boxes. Sow tomatoes (for a heated crop), aubergines, broad and French beans in fibre pots. Gloxinia and sweet pea seeds should also be sown in fibre pots. Don't forget to water pot plants – keep the compost moist, not sodden. Give dahlia tubers warmth to encourage sprouting before taking cuttings. Put in chrysanthemum cuttings. Begin to water and gently heat pots of fuchsia, hippeastrum and other dormant plants to stimulate growth. Pot up strong calceolaria seedlings and prick out those sown for late blooming. Re-pot any plants whose roots have outgrown their pots.

Don't forget

To start early potatoes at the end of the month; to plan the annual and perennial planting for the season ahead. Get catalogues and order seeds and plants well in advance to avoid disappointment. New gladioli corms and alpine plants should be ordered now in time for the delivery and planting in early spring.

Visits

By definition botanic gardens tend to display a rich living catalogue of plants. So it is there that gardeners can often learn which are the species which offer the most joy in bleak months or possess the most notable dormant features – berries, bark or an unsuspectedly beautiful twig tracery.

Botanic gardens in cities like Bath, Birmingham, Bristol, Cambridge, Durham, Edinburgh, Liverpool, Oxford and Sheffield as well as the Royal Gardens at Kew or the Arboreta at Westonbirt in Gloucestershire and Flimwell in Kent are all places where gardeners can learn lots of lessons about offsetting winter drabness.

WINTER WARMTH

Most of us would like a bright, frost-free area in which to overwinter plants like rooted geranium cuttings, or to bring on tomato plants and other early salad crops. The problem is that the cost of heating the whole greenhouse is prohibitively expensive.

An excellent solution is to make a mini-hothouse inside an unheated glasshouse. Only basic tools and no great skills are required to make the sort of simple construction shown in our drawing. First, you'll need an old table or bench to put it on, which you should top with an insulating sheet of thick glass-fibre-coated roofing felt to prevent heat loss from below. Heating cables and thermostats, necessary to keep the sand base and the air in the mini-house well above freezing, are made by several companies and widely advertised in gardening magazines.

Safety must always be uppermost in your mind when you lay out the heating cable. Never allow it to cross or otherwise touch itself, or it will overheat. The sand base should always be kept moist (not drenched) to allow the conduction of heat; you can make sure of this by spending a little extra on an automatically-fed capilliary mat to lay beneath the sand. When the seed trays or pots have been set on the sand base, the surface areas between them should be topped with a half-inch layer of damp peat to spread the heat.

As a rough guide a mini-house providing 15 sq ft of standing space needs approximately 80 ft of cable, and to run it in cold weather costs around 45p a week. This means a lettuce could be grown in winter for as little as 6p; bedding plants at 15p a box, and tomato plants in individual pots at 3p each.

Gardeners rich or dedicated enough to heat the *whole* greenhouse can cut their

The do-it-yourself mini-hothouse. Vital ingredients: polythene sheet-clad walls and roof (1) supported on a simple wooden frame (a similar sheet lines the base); heating cables (2) sandwiched in a 3-inch layer of sand (3); a layer of moist peat (4) to spread the heat, controlled by a thermostat (5); glass-fibre-coated roofing felt (6) for bottom insulation

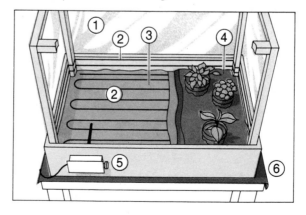

gas, oil or electricity bills by lining the house with insulating plastic sheets. The commonest kind is a double layer of transparent plastic with air bubbles trapped in between. It comes either on a roll or in tailored kits.

THE SLOPING SALAD BED

A solid south-west-facing garden wall makes a wonderful prop for a sloping salad bed. One of gardening's oldest gimmicks, this method of growing accelerates such crops as spring onion, lettuce, beetroot, radish and even strawberries.

Seeds or plants are spaced normally on a 40-degree slope, facing south west. This ensures that the developing crops obtain maximum solar radiation. Early or late in the season this can advance harvesting by a week or more.

The base for a salad slope is made by packing hardcore, builder's rubble or coarse clinker to a height of 4ft 6in from a base line 5ft 3in out from a strong wall. The base must be really firm to prevent slipping, but its surface should remain sufficiently rough and porous to ensure good drainage. The top of the base should be semi-sealed with finer material to prevent the soil washing through.

Once levelled to an even 40-degree slope, the base should be covered with at least 6in of good loam and allowed to settle for a few days before planting. The final bed can be any length, but 6ft is a useful working minimum. Crops can be further advanced by means of cloches.

Provided the drainage is good and the soil surface is kept lightly cultivated, soil-wash down the slope can be kept to a minimum. But to restore the correct soil depth over the slope when preparing for planting in spring, digging with a fork should be carried out parallel to the wall – starting at the top and moving the soil upwards.

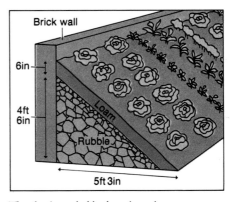

The sloping salad bed, an ingenious way to accelerate the growth of crops like spring onion, lettuce, beetroot, radish and strawberries, by exposing them to the maximum amount of sunlight

PLANTS OF THE MONTH

TREES

Acacia dealbata – bright yellow tiny globes in warm districts.

Alnus incana 'Aurea' – red tinted catkins.

SHRUBS

Lonicera fragrantissima – creamy white, scented flowers.

Camellia sasanqua – small fragrant white flowers.

Garrya elliptica – large bright catkins.

Mahonia 'Charity' – chains of lemon yellow flowers.

Viburnum tinus – white flowers.

Clematis cirrhosa – bell-shaped flowers.

BORDER PLANTS

Cyclamen coum – pink, crimson and white flowers.

Helleborus niger – white 'Christmas roses'.

Primula vulgaris – the enchanting common yellow primrose.

Iris unguicularis – fragrant lilac blue flowers.

Helleborus x corsicus – pale green flower cups.

February

Brighter skies at the end of the month will remind us that the gardening world is waking up. The days will be getting longer, and the increased light will be energizing the plants into action. The first green spears of new growth will be pushing up from the crowns of established perennials in the flower beds, and the buds of deciduous shrubs will become obviously fatter.

This is when gardeners will begin to panic. Now they realise just how much winter work they have neglected, and in trying to make up for lost time will fill the country's physiotherapy departments with badly overstrained lower backs. Wise gardeners will get on with the heavy work from the beginning of the month and take it steadily. The saying for February is 'Two half loads in the barrow equals steady progress. One excessive load equals a busted back.'

Ground work

Finish all major digging as soon as possible, but work only on dry days. When-ever weather permits, finish spreading as much organic material as possible (compost, spent hops, well-rotted manure etc.) on to the open ground in the vegetable patch, forking it well into the topsoil. Break down and level the soil on previously treated areas so that it is ready to be broken down further to make suitable sowing drills towards the end of the month.

Bury a thick layer of compost or manure one spit below the soil surface along the lines where maincrop onions will be grown, and pull up the soil to form a low ridge along the line where early-sown peas are beginning to emerge. Make new strawberry beds by digging in an extra load of manure or compost on the planting site. If you are planning to sow any new areas of lawn next month, begin now by carefully raking the soil level. Draw a long stout wooden board across the surface to reveal undulations that need flattening.

Keep hoeing or forking out emerging weed seedlings wherever you spot them – they are much easier to remove when the subsoil is moist. Make the 'weed patrol' a disciplined routine, arming yourself with a bucket and either a long-handled fork or a narrow border fork. Extend your attention to the bog garden and curb the exuberance of species like rushes, grasses, watermints and buttercups. Fork out sections of the larger clumps, otherwise some of the prettier flowering plants will be deprived of vital space.

Now is the time to finish major construction work on paths, terraces, pergolas and ponds. If you leave it any later there will not be time for this year's planting to soften the impression of newness.

Pruning

Cut back summer-flowering clematis hybrids to leave about 6in of woody stem; cut away to old wood last year's shoots of established wall shrubs like *Campsis radicans*, spirea and tamarisk; and cut back the shoots of winter sweet and winter jasmine which have flowered this year. Thin out old or weak wood in wall plants like solanum or summer-flowering jasmine; trim and train climber and rambler roses; finish pruning fruit trees and cut back the canes of autumn-fruiting raspberries.

Security

Spray simazine-based weedkiller around established trees, shrubs and roses to protect them from weed competition later. Make wall supports for recently planted climbers like honeysuckles which need something to cling on to. I like to use strands of ex-army field telephone wire (often advertised in gardening magazines). Fit it in parallel horizontals 18in apart, attaching it to nails or screws placed at approximate 9ft intervals. If this is too much bother, you can use the new plastic ties which you stick to the wall with resin putty. They are much more effective than they look. At the end of the month spray peaches, nectarines and apricots twice (leave a ten-day interval) with copper fungicide to prevent leaf curl.

Cleaning and tidying

Sort out pea and bean canes, and make sure you have enough. Find a source of twiggy young hazel or hawthorn branches to use as supports for low-growing pea varieties. Clear the vegetable patch of everything which isn't still cropping well, and bend the leaves over the flowers on the remaining broccoli plants to protect them from heavy frost.

Take the sprayer apart and wash the components very thoroughly in detergent and washing soda, concentrating particularly on hoses, nozzles and filters. Oil all moving parts.

Outdoor planting

Finish dividing and replanting large clumps of perennials like Michaelmas daisy and golden rod. Move any young shrubs or clumps of perennials which you have now realised are in the wrong place. Plant hardy roses, new delphiniums, anemones and ranunculus.

Outdoor sowing

Towards the end of the month sow patches of the herbaceous border with

Coronilla valentina glauca, with its bright
yellow flowers and evergreen foliage – a half
hardy shrub that will reach 3½ to 4½ ft against
a protective wall or fence.

the seed of ten-week stock. Sow the next batches of peas, beans, lettuce, beetroot and radish, and make the major sowings of sprouts (for autumn crop), early cabbage, carrots, onions, leeks, spring onions, garlic, seakale, parsley and Chinese cabbage. Young seedlings will appreciate any protection – like cloches – you can give.

Feeding

Top dress the herbaceous border with a tablespoon of Growmore complete fertiliser sprinkled around each clump and lightly scuffled into the topsoil with a handfork. Lightly hoe round roses, then apply a thick mulch of manure or compost around the stems. Give all trees and shrubs a dressing of coated slow-release fertiliser forked into the ground in the area shaded by their leaf canopies. Scatter 4oz hydrated lime per square yard over areas of the vegetable plot which received an early dressing of manure. Dust earthed-up rows of peas with hydrated lime.

Lawn work

Spread worm control preparations on evenings which seem likely to be followed by a mild night. Try to improve the drainage of mossy areas by close deep forking, then treat with mercurised lawn sand. At the end of the month spread worm casts by sweeping with a besom.

Pick off any hard objects like stones and give the grass its first spring mowing (with the blades set high).

Maintenance

Make sure the chains and supports for hanging baskets are in good condition. Scrape, rust-proof and paint where necessary. Examine the structure and mounting of window-boxes and carry out any repairs or painting necessary so that they are ready for planting next month.

In the greenhouse

Sow antirrhinums, begonias, lobelias, petunias, verbenas, pyrethrums and tobaccos in boxes to produce plants for summer bedding. Expose boxes of plants like cauliflowers and lettuces to the air outside to begin hardening off for transplanting early next month. Bring them inside only if frost is forecast. Thin onions previously sown in boxes.

Take geranium and chrysanthemum cuttings and set them in moist compost around the edges of large clay pots. Alternatively, root them in holes in small blocks of Oasis foam. Re-pot ferns and fuchsias which have become rootbound. Sow bush tomatoes to produce plants for use outdoors later – 3in fibre pots or the cavities in Propapaks are ideal.

Mix rotted compost, chopped straw and fresh animal manure in equal proportions with good loam soil and build the mix into an 18in deep, 3ft by 3ft rectangle in a cold frame or corner of the greenhouse. When it has fermented, heated up and begun to cool down again this will make a fine bed later in the year for cucumbers, melons, squashes, marrows and courgettes.

Don't forget

To obtain supplies of fertiliser, pesticide etc. which you will need throughout the season; to order any bulbs, shrubs or other plants which you have admired in other gardens during the winter; to plan exactly what you intend to do with pots, planters, hanging baskets and window-boxes, and order all the plants you will require.

Visits

The original intentions of garden designers can best be appreciated in gardens which depend heavily upon their structure for their appeal before they have been masked by an abundance of flower and foliage. This means that February, which is often considered an unattractive month to be out and about, may offer some of the richest rewards to people interested in garden architecture; with plants at their most subdued all the flaws and most of the genius are revealed.

Stourhead, near Stourton, Wiltshire; Dartington Hall, Buckfastleigh, Devon;

Hampton Court, Sunbury, Surrey; Studley Royal, near Rippon, Yorkshire; the University of York; Packwood House, Lapworth, Warwickshire; Rousham, Lower Heyford, Oxfordshire; Lyme Hall, Stockport, Cheshire; Port Meirion, near Port Madoc, Gwynedd and Pollok House, Glasgow all merit February visits.

SUPER SOWING

One good way of hastening the establishment of seeds is to pregerminate them and then sow them in a fluid. It is easy to do, and all you need is a plastic sandwich box, some soft non-medicated toilet tissue, a paper towel, a polythene bag and a packet of non-fungicidal cellulose wallpaper paste.

Lay the paper in the bottom of the box – several layers of toilet tissue first; then the paper towel – to make a lining. Flood it with water and tip away the excess. Then sprinkle the seeds evenly over the paper, put the top on the box and keep it at a temperature of approximately 70°F (kitchen or living-room temperature). Examine the seeds every day: when most of them have a ¼in of root (for most vegetables this will take between two and four days) they are ready to sow. If necessary, they will keep for a few days in the salad compartment of the fridge.

To prepare the sowing medium, mix the paste to approximately half the normal wallpapering strength. About a

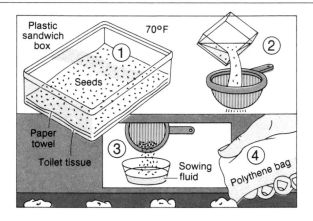

quarter-pint of fluid will be needed to sow every 30ft of drill.

Wash the germinated seed from the sandwich box into a fine strainer taking care not to finger them. Pour half the sowing fluid into a bowl and sprinkle with the seed; then add the rest of the fluid and stir gently until the seeds are evenly mixed. The sowing is done with the clear polythene bag, used like an icing-bag with one corner snipped off to make a nozzle. With only a little practice, it is easy to 'spot' sow a single seed in a gobbet of the fluid.

SOCIAL CLIMBING

One of the gardener's most pleasing and enjoyable achievements is to grow plants in unusual ways. Our Victorian ancestors used to do wonderful things with vigorous climbing plants, making them adopt all sorts of forms. Among the prettiest pieces of garden manipulation was to make normally wall-dependent climbers

like wisteria become small standard trees.

If you follow the instructions on the drawing you will, in four years, convert a young wisteria into a passable tree.

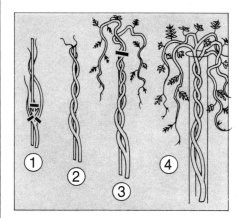

(1) After planting prune the stems away to leave two good buds. (2) Twine together the stems which emerge from these buds as they grow – removing any side shoots which might develop. (3) Prune the top of the twined main shoots at 8ft above the ground just above good buds to encourage bushing. (4) Provide good support for the developing 'crown'

PLANTS OF THE MONTH
TREES
Magnolia campbellii – pink petalled flowers.

Salix aegyptiaca – bright yellow catkins.

SHRUBS
Daphne mezereum – strongly scented purple flowers.

Skimmia japonica rubella – pinkish white scented flowers.

Chimonanthus praecox – scented creamy flowered 'winter sweet'.

Cornus mas – small yellow tufted flowers.

Pachysansdra terminalis – greenish flowers.

Coronilla valentina glauca – bright yellow flowers.

BORDER PLANTS
Galanthus atkinsii – a stately snowdrop.

Rananculus ficaria flore plena – golden yellow double celandine flowers.

Cyclamen persicum – large pale pink or white flowers with red centres.

Helleborus foetidus – bright green flowers.

Crocus aureus – golden yellow cups.

March

This is the most critical month. Omissions now will become glaringly obvious later. Final land preparation, sowing and planting lend a satisfying sense of order which, though a trifle bleak to look at, will rapidly vanish in the surge of spring growth.

Ground work

All land previously dug and left rough should be dug with a fork and levelled with a rake. Remove weeds. Areas to be sown or planted up should have a second cross-raking to achieve a fine-crumbed tilth.

Make new asparagus beds. Choose a warm southern aspect sheltered from the wind. Dig over clay soils to about 2ft deep, adding as much rotted manure or compost as possible to the top foot. Well-drained sandy or gravelly soils should be dug and manured down to 4ft deep. Add organic material to raise the level of the beds, which should be 5ft wide separated by 2ft wide alleys. Some of the topsoil from the alleys can be piled on the beds to increase the ridge effect. Asparagus beds are worth the effort –

they can last 100 years.

Dig and prepare planting holes for any trees and shrubs still to plant. If you plan to build a permanent barbecue, start now. Its supporting walls can be brick or stone. You need stout metal mesh for fire support and grill, which should sit on metal brackets cemented into the walls. Finish work on paths, steps, terraces etc.

Pruning

At the end of the month cut away rose stems damaged by frost and cut back bush roses to four or five strong stems about 6in long, making an oblique cut just above an outward pointing bud. Similarly leave only 3 or 4in of last year's stems on the crowns of standard roses. Don't just hack away blindly. Consider the shape that the crown may develop after pruning and whether stems might conflict with one another. Side shoots can be amputated later. Finish all shrub pruning.

After tying last year's new main-crop raspberry, blackberry and loganberry canes on to support wires snip away an inch or two of their growing points, disinfecting the secateurs by wiping with a rag soaked in Jeyes fluid between cuts.

Security

In mid-month carry out the pre-budburst insecticidal and fungicidal spraying of fruit trees. Repeat at ten to fourteen days intervals on apples and pears through much of spring and summer if large crops of unblemished fruit are required. Follow the instructions. Don't spray insecticides when bees are active on fruit blossom or when useful predators like ladybirds are around. If in adverse seasons you can accept small crops of blemished fruit you need not spray at all. A good compromise is to spray only when a particular pest or disease is threatening damage.

Cover the blossom on wall fruit against late frost and birds with plastic sheet, cut bracken or fronds of evergreen trees. Treat snails and slugs around emerging seedlings with slug bait pellets or 'slug pubs', which will drown the creatures in beer. Finish weedkilling paths, drives, etc. Be careful of nearby plants. Moss is easily controlled with tar oil wash applied by a watering can with a rose head.

Outdoor planting

Make sure early potatoes are sprouting well because by the end of the month they should be planted out. Rub away any long and weak shoots, leaving two or three stout shoots per seed. Nestle them about 4in below the surface. On well-manured ground they can be planted at 9in intervals in rows 9in apart. By August they should then produce uniform, pearly-skinned tubers about the size of bantam's eggs.

Divide and transplant alpines. Plant out carnations, chrysanthemums, gladiolus, pansies, violas and pot-sown sweet peas. Lift, separate and replant mint and chives. Plant out hardened-off, pot-sown early peas. Plant horseradish, Jerusalem artichokes and asparagus crowns at the end of the month. Plant out new bush fruit including any rooted cuttings. Plant strawberries.

If you haven't already done it, get your second early potatoes to sprout by mid-month and main crop potatoes to follow two weeks later.

Outdoor sowing

Sow hardy annuals like clarkias, coreopsis cosmos, larkspur, godetia, gypsophila,

Narcissus bulbocodium – this teeny-bopper among the daffodils is one of the prettiest and least usual. Since their 'hooped petticoats' curtsy in the spring from only 6in above the ground they are best displayed in raised beds, pots or by nestling them round the bole of a tree

lavatera, poppies and sweet peas in prepared areas of the flower beds. Later in the month sow lupins, nigella, alyssum, nasturtium, calendula, campanulas, Chinese asters, sunflowers and stocks. Sow directly into patches of the herb garden chervil, chives, dill, marjoram, parsley and sorrel.

Carry out major sowings in the vegetable plot. The final spacing of the plants which should be sown now is show in brackets: broad beans (9in in rows 9in apart); broccoli (24in in rows 24in apart); Brussel sprouts (24in 30 in); winter cabbage (18in 24in); carrots (4in 4in); cauli-

flower (18in 24in); lettuce (9in 9in); dwarf beans (6in 6in); kale (24in 24in); onions (9in 9in); parsnips (9in 9in); corn salad (9in 9in); peas (3in 9in); spinach (9in 9in); turnips and swedes (6in 6in). Sow seeds more closely in the row than the final spacing and thin out twice as they develop to leave the strongest plants. Onion thinnings can be used in salads. To save space in the vegetable plot early in the season, brassicas, which need a wide final spacing, can be sown more closely in nursery beds and then transplanted in June or July in rows at their final spacing.

Further short rows of radish (1in in rows 1in apart) and salad onions (1in 1in) should also be sown at the end of the month to ensure continuity of supply.

Feeding

Prepare dahlia beds by removing the top 4in of soil and spreading a 4in layer of manure or compost plus 3oz per sq yd of bonemeal. Replace the topsoil and fork the bed down to 18in, mixing the manure with the soil. Give a general dressing with Growmore fertiliser to areas of the herbaceous beds ignored last month. You can make a single application to feed the beds all season with the coated slow release (six months) formulations. More expensive initially, they are cheaper in the long run.

Lawn work

Sow new lawn areas by the end of the month to allow seed to establish before the drier weather. A week before sowing broadcast 2oz per square yard of Growmore fertiliser. When the topsoil has been raked to as fine and level a surface as possible compact it on a dry day by heavily treading down. Get your family and friends stamping hard. Check the levels again by rubbing a long, stout, wooden board over the area to reveal all hills and hollows. Rake level and tread again.

Using a spring tine rake, gently scrape the compacted surface in one direction only. Broadcast evenly 4oz per square yard of fine lawn seed and then cover it by scraping with the spring tine wire rake, moving at 90 degrees to the previous raking. If rain doesn't fall within two days, fine-hose the sown area for long, gentle moistening.

Sow grass seed to repair bare patches in the established lawn after forking the soil well and breaking up the top with a rake. Feed established lawns with 1oz sulphate of potash and ½oz nitrate of soda per square yard. Mix the fertilisers with an equal volume of fine sharp sand to make even broadcasting easier. Water in well. Spray with lawn weedkiller.

Maintenance

Check nuts and bolts to ensure mower doesn't shed metal on the lawn.

In the greenhouse

Pot on azaleas, camellia, marguerite, fuchsia and geranium cuttings when their roots have well-developed. Prick off begonias sown last month into 3in fibre pots or the cavities in polystyrene trays. Start to harden well-developed bedding plants. Sow ageratum, antirrhinum, celosia, freesia, gloxinia, hollyhocks, pansy. At the end of the month sow alyssum, anchusa, arabis, calceolaria, nemesia, nicotiana, tagetes and zinnias. Prick off January-sown leeks.

Sow melon, marrow and squashes: two seeds per 3in fibre pot but single out after germination, leaving the strongest seedling. Sow tomato seed for an unheated greenhouse crop. Sow basil in a seed box. Start feeding and giving more water to house plants. Pot them on if rootbound.

Don't forget

When building the barbecue, leave enough surface for standing dishes and preparing food.

Weedkiller can creep after heavy rain affecting susceptible plants.

Visits

Even though your garden at home may only just be emerging from its winter torpor this is a fine month to take encouragement from the wonders which serious gardeners have contrived in our great gardens.

Athelhampton in Dorset; Berkeley Castle in Gloucestershire; Bowood, near Chippenham, in Wiltshire; Lanhydrock in Cornwall; Ascott Gardens, near Leighton Buzzard, Bedfordshire; Hever Castle in Kent; Savill Garden, near Windsor, Berkshire; Harlow Car, near Harrogate, Yorkshire; Crathes Castle, Banchory, Grampian; Birr Castle, Co. Offaly; Anne's Grove, Castletownroach, Co. Cork; Garinish Island, Glengariff, Co. Cork and many others offer delightful evidence of the spring awakening.

SUPER-CLOCHE

Even without a glasshouse, exotic vegetables like peppers (capsicums) or aubergines can be grown in the garden. But if they are to produce worthwhile crops in cool seasons they must have protection from the worst of the weather until they are very well grown – which is the perfect argument for the colossal cloche.

Producing a cloche to the design shown here takes less than an hour and costs very little.

Thanks to the fact that the twin-ply covering sheets are reinforced by a woven plastic net sandwich between them they don't tear, and they are stabilised against ultra-violet rays, so don't crack either. Simple watering can be provided by running a seep hose down the cloche when

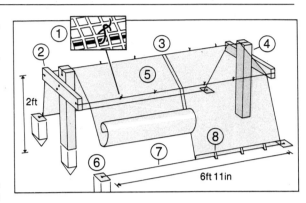

The Super-cloche; easily built cover for plants which need to grow tall. Use twist ties to hold the reinforced plastic sheet (5) to the wire (1) stretched between 3in by 1in cross-members (2) at 2ft above the ground. These are supported by two 3in square hardwood posts (4). The covering sheets should overlap by 1in (3). The 3in square hardwood stakes (6), with the strong supporting wire attached (7), should lie flush with ground level to allow the sheeting to be held down by clothes pegs (8)

planting, or the holding pegs can be removed and the side panels rolled up to allow watering.

Apart from crops which absolutely need the extra heat, crops such as courgettes and tomatoes also prosper much better if they are grown in a large cloche initially. All plants thrive better when protected from cold winds and even a foot-high hedge of plastic supported by stakes round the edge of a vegetable plot will allow young plants to develop much faster. And a sheet of plastic held on to a wall by a wooden batten attached with masonry nails can be rolled down to create a lean-to house to protect tomatoes in their early stages and prevent too much heat loss.

THE PERFECT COMPOST HEAP

You don't need anything more complicated than an old packing case to make good compost for the garden, and now,

at the beginning of the growing season when more and more compostable material will be produced, is a good time to start the first batch.

Compost is the result of the natural rotting of mixed plant and animal material. It takes place in a moist, warm, airy environment. The process is assisted by micro-organisms, fungi and small animals.

Starters, such as well-rotted animal manure, help to speed composting during cold weather. They encourage the multiplication of micro-organisms which decompose the organic matter. A simple mixture of sulphate of ammonia and ground chalk is as good as a proprietary starter. In summer it takes three months to make compost but in autumn and winter it may take twice as long. When the heap is finished it needs a lid to keep the heat in – this is vital to the composting process. The lid should be permeable, old sacks or carpets are ideal.

The perfect compost heap. Over a layer of raw material (2) add a half-inch soil layer, with a sprinkling of lime if the soil is acid city soil (3); then over another layer of raw material add a starter layer (1) of manure and fertiliser

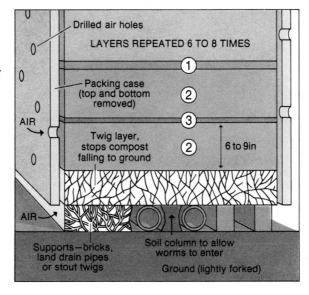

It is also vital to turn compost thoroughly once a month. Old hands have at least two containers so that they can fork the maturing compost from one to the other, mixing it in the process. Air is essential; materials which pack too tightly and exclude air, such as leaves or lawn clippings, should be well mixed with other bulky materials.

Humus is what comes from a well-made compost heap. It contains minerals, gums which help stick sand particles in the soil, and other colloids which help very fine clay particles to remain apart. The major materials are calcium, nitrogen, potassium, phosphorous – all essential to plant growth. The gums and colloids improve the physical nature of the soil and build up a crumbly structure which makes cultivation easier. Improved soil structure allows free air and water movement so important to plant growth.

The best way to use compost is to work it into the soil lightly, and also to spread it as a moisture-conserving mulch on top of the soil.

It is virtually impossible to apply too much compost to the garden. Use an old packing case to make a compost heap as shown in the diagram.

PLANTS OF THE MONTH

TREES

Sorbus megalocarpa – white flowers before bud burst followed by brown fruit.

Prunus dulcis – the pink flowered common almond.

SHRUBS

Azara microphylla – scented yellow flowers.

Spiraea thunbergii – arching sprays of white flowers.

Viburnum bodnantense – scented white flowers.

Pieris floribunda – cream lily of the valley flowers.

BORDER PLANTS

Bergenia 'Silver Light' – pinkish white flowers.

Cyclamen balearicum – fragrant white flowers.

Iris unguicularis 'Lazica' – dark purple, white marked flowers.

Narcissus cyclamineus – baby yellow daffodils.

Pulmonaria angustifolia azurea – bright blue flowers.

April

This is the month when work avoided on chillier days will have to be completed. Look back at your almanac and catch up, regardless of the weather. But remember that for sowing seed or setting out plants it is the temperature and the weather prospects, rather than the date, which is important – the almanac can only be a general guide.

If you live in the north or some of the higher, more exposed areas of the midlands and south your work programme may well be two to three weeks behind that of gardeners in balmier areas.

Ground work

Complete any digging and levelling of beds required for the coming season. A flush of annual weeds will begin to show on previously cultivated ground and among established plants. Attack relentlessly. Whether you choose to hoe from on high or go in for close combat with the long-handled hand fork, have them out as soon as they show their heads. Collect their wilting relics in a bucket or barrow for compost. Otherwise spring showers may encourage them to re-root.

Pruning

When autumn- and spring-flowering trees and shrubs have finished blooming cut away any damaged, very old or weak branches and twigs and take the chance to shape them for the coming year. Cut forsythia back to within two buds of the old wood. It is also a good time to tidy evergreens such as euonymus, lavender, *Magnolia grandiflora*, olearia or evergreen viburnums.

Cut back to ground level the old stems of rambler roses which flowered last season. Leave only four or five of the strongest new stems to flower this year.

Remove any very old and damaged stems of climbing roses and select a few young branches to be allowed to grow on to replace them. Cut back all the remaining side branches to within 4in of the main stems, cutting obliquely across them just beyond a bud. Shorten the main stems by a few inches.

When pruning don't let the 'rules' overcome the aesthetics – remember the overall picture you are trying to create. If you rely on climbing plants to cover the lower areas of a wall you might leave old stems which you would otherwise remove to provide leaf and bloom for a further year while young replacements are developing. Don't become a clip-o-maniac.

Security

April starts the period of the pest vigil. As soon as they realise that plants are waking up and there is plenty of juicy grub about, the pests begin to rampage. Keep your eye open for habitual scourges like slugs and greenflies. Bait to attract the slugs. If you can protect slug bait pellets from rain they will remain effective for longer. Slug 'pubs', which use beer to attract and drown them, are worth trying.

Your fruit spraying routine should now be well established for the apples and pears. It consists of a systemic fungicidal spray every fortnight with insecticide included as appropriate. Aphids, suckers, capsids, caterpillars, apple-leaf miner and apple blossom weevil can all attack now.

The tiny, reddish-brown, moving specks on the lower surface of leaves which have begun to crinkle and turn a bronzish colour are red spiders. Allowed to prosper they will reduce the crop. If you see them, include a systemic insecticide in the routine spray. By the end of the month the apple flower buds should be turning pink and that's the time mildew begins to attack. In addition to the second application of systemic fungicide, prune away any buds and foliage showing the tell-tale white powder. Begin spraying roses with fungicide to control blackspot and mildew.

As soon as the flowers begin to open, spray gooseberries to control mildew with systemic fungicide and repeat the treatment three times at fortnightly intervals. Cut out obviously infected shoots. A similar treatment should also protect strawberries from grey mould and mildew.

The best way of preventing birds from pecking away at the succulent young shoots emerging from seeds is to cover them with low 'tunnels' made by bending fine gauge wire-mesh. When planting out brassica seedlings soak their roots in a club root dip.

This is a good time to sprinkle a soil insecticide alongside rows of newly planted or sown vegetables to control such pests as cabbage root fly, wireworms, millepedes and leather jackets.

April doesn't always turn out to be a damp month. So be sure that young plants don't collapse through lack of water.

Outdoor planting

Plant out second early potatoes by mid-month and main crop potatoes at the end of the month. Space the latter at 15in intervals in rows 30in apart.

Plant out brassicas, rhubarb, courgettes, (at 2ft intervals, preferably under cloches), sage, thyme and marjoram. Plant out onions started indoors. Set them as shallow as possible while still remaining firmly in the ground.

Plant out pot-raised broad beans in

Anenome blanda – with attractive deeply cut
foliage, smart dark stems and a mass of cheery
daisies, when it begins to flower it banishes the
wintery feeling from herbaceous borders.

double rows set 9in apart. Space the young plants at 9in intervals with those in one row standing opposite the middles of the gaps in the other. Further double rows can be planted at a distance of 24in.

Plant out first leeks at the end of the month 3in down in 6in deep pockets of compost-enriched soil. Harden off and plant out previously pricked-out bedding plants. Plant out violas, montbretia, pot-sown sweet peas, carnations, gladiolus, lobelia, dahlia and pricked-out and hardened-off antirrhinums at the end of the month. Pinch out the central stems from the antirrhinums to make them bush out.

Outdoor sowing

Sow additional rows of radish and lettuce between the planted brassicas. Sow pickling onions thinly and garlic bulbils at 6in intervals. By the end of the month sow the seed of half-hardy annual flowers.

Feeding

Clad the soil around roses with a mulch of peat or well-rotted compost or manure at least 2in thick. Apply fertiliser between rows of emerging early potatoes and protect their young foliage by drawing a little soil up around it with a rake.

Lawn work

This is the latest time that either laying turf or sowing seed to create new lawn is sensible. It should be carried out only if there is good provision for watering in case a dry spell follows planting.

By the end of the month lawns sown in March could need their first cut if the grass has grown to 4in. Before cutting, consolidate the soil surface with a light roller and allow a couple of days for the grass to grow erect again. If possible use a rotary mower set at least 2in from the soil surface for the first cut.

General outdoor work

Support early-sown dwarf peas with twigs retained from previous pruning. Push their mainstems firmly into the ground and allow them to emerge to 6in above the advertised height of the variety.

Established asparagus should be ready for cropping by the end of the month. Do the job carefully with a sharp, long and narrow-bladed knife. Cut the spears when they are about 5in long, cutting close to the crown beneath the soil.

In the greenhouse

As temperatures rise, more frequent watering and feeding plus careful attention to ventilation will be necessary from now until the autumn. Liquid-feed any house plants as they begin to bloom. The end of the month is a good time to reproduce softwood plants by rooting cuttings indoors.

Young tomato plants should be set in growbags by the end of month. Remove all side shoots from the leaf axils as they develop. Strings to the glasshouse roof or long canes forced into the ground through the bags can be used to support the vines as they grow.

Sow seed for outdoor bush tomatoes on compost in boxes and pot up the seedlings, into individual 3in pots, as soon as true leaves develop. Try to prevent whitefly developing by treating the house with a permethrin-based smoke generator. Keep an eye open for red spider and stamp it out with a systemic insecticide. Begin regular fungicidal spraying. Pot on basil plants and prick out previously sown annuals. Sow phlox, petunia, stocks and other half-hardy annuals. At the end of the month establish melon, marrow, squash and cucumber plants on previously prepared beds.

Visits

Between the middle of this month and the middle of May gardens with acid soils which have been planted with a spring display in mind offer rhododendrons and azaleas at their best. If you want to enjoy them you should plan carefully in advance because it is astonishing how quickly they pass their peak.

Trengwainton near Penzance, Cornwall; Knighthayes Court, Tiverton, Devon; Hergest Croft, Kington, Herefordshire; Exbury Gardens, Beaulieu, Hampshire; Leonards Lee, Horsham, Sussex; Nymans, Handcross, Sussex; Newstead Abbey, Ravenshead, Nottinghamshire; Lingholme, near Keswick, Cumbria; Craggside, Rothbury, Northumberland; Crarae Lodge, Inverary, Strathclyde offer among the best of the spring pageants.

RAISED BEDS

It is not too late to think of growing your vegetable and salad crops in raised beds; these are much more productive than ordinary ground and most suitable for gardeners with only the minimum of space available.

Raised beds are double dug areas on which the original soil is enriched by adding well-rotted organic matter in a 1:1 ratio. The additional 'soil' is held in place by edging each 4ft by 4ft bed with stout boards held in place by pickets (see diagram). If the beds are separated by 1½ft paths the centre of the beds can be reached without putting a foot on their surface.

Beds like this both drain and retain water so well and are so rich that salad and vegetable crops can be grown on them at practically twice the density at which they can be grown on ordinary open ground.

This denser planting and thorough initial digging greatly reduce the weed competition and therefore the need for weeding. The dense ground cover which it provides cuts down the surface evaporation of soil moisture and therefore the need for watering in the summer.

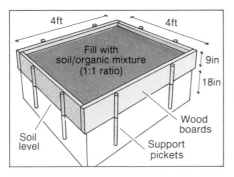

RING-CULTURE

Even if you only have a patch of concrete or a tiny balcony, it is surprising how many tomatoes you can grow with the ring-culture technique. It most easily provides the amateur with all requirements for a successful crop. Water is supplied regularly by capillary action from a gravel bed as the plants need it. This is easily made by laying a 500-gauge plastic sheet on the ground (preferably alongside a south-facing wall which will store heat and reflect the sun) and raising its edges over strips of wood or lines of brick to form a shallow trough 4in deep by 27in wide and long enough to accommodate plants spaced at 18in intervals (four is a reasonable minimum to grow).

The trough is filled with a 4in layer of ⅛in to ¼in washed gravel, obtainable from most builder's merchants. If gravel is hard to obtain, peat may be used.

Young tomato seedlings (preferably showing their first truss of flowers) are planted into 9in diameter bottomless pots (the rings) in a John Innes No. 3

It's surprising how many tomatoes you can grow with the ring-culture technique. Make a trough on the ground or a bench by cradling a polythene sheet (1) inside a frame of wood or bricks (7). Fill the trough with a 4in layer of gravel or peat. Plant the tomato in a bottomless 'ring-culture' pot (2) filled with John Innes No. 3 compost (3). Nestle the pot into the gravel or peat base and force a 5ft stake (4) down through the ring to the bottom of the trough. The feeding roots (5) will seek out the nutrient in the compost while the drinking roots (6) will move down into the base to absorb water initially and dissolved nutrients later

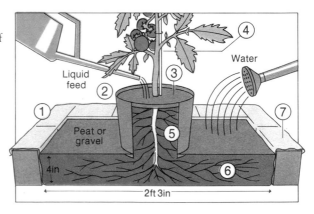

compost. It is best to half fill the ring with compost, place the seedling on top and then pack more compost round its roots. The rings should be stood along the centre of the trough and gently seated half an inch into the gravel. A 5ft cane or stake (to which the growing plant can be lightly tied later) should be firmly pushed through the compost in the ring to the base of the trough.

Initially both ring and gravel should be soaked in water. For the next month (unless the young plants are obviously wilting) only the gravel need be kept constantly moist. During that time the base fertilisers in the compost will be sought out by the developing feeder root system inside the ring. Meanwhile a separate root system will spread down into the gravel to provide more solid anchorage and be ready to absorb the vast quantities of water needed during cropping.

After the first month, as well as keeping the gravel topped up with water, a dose of liquid fertiliser should be supplied weekly to the ring. Once the fourth truss of fruit has set, this food supplement should be applied twice weekly until cropping ends.

PLANTS OF THE MONTH

TREES

Pyrus salicifolia 'Pendula' – delicate weeping, white flowered, ornamental pear.

Magnolia stellata – fragrant white flowers.

SHRUBS

Osmanthus x burkwoodii – perfumed tubular white flowers.

Camellia x williamsii 'Bow Bells' – bright rose flowers.

Viburnum tinus variegatum – white flowers and variegated leaves.

Azara microphylla – small yellow flowers which smell of vanilla.

BORDER PLANTS

Anemone blanda – dark stems and daisies.

Primula denticulata – violet round flower heads.

Vinca major variegata – blue flowered periwinkle with variegated leaves.

Brunnera macrophylla variegata – boldly variegated leaves and bright blue flowers.

Pulsatilla vulgaris – violet flowered.

Pulmonaria 'Munstead Blue' – variegated leaves and strong blue flowers.

May

This month you'll need to continue the outdoor sowing of flowers and vegetables and complete the planting-out of seedlings raised indoors. Care in watering is essential. Until their roots are well established, young plants can suffer terribly in dry spells. Keep an eye on the topsoil and water whenever it starts to become dry and powdery. Sprinkle very slowly through a fine rose, kept constantly moving to ensure even distribution and prevent puddling.

Ground work

When the top growth of potatoes has reached approximately 9in, begin to earth up by raking topsoil around the stems from the middle of the furrows. Also stir up the soil around globe artichokes and reduce the number of main shoots per plant to three.

Hoe regularly to cut out weeds and keep the soil loose around all developing crops, and thin out seedlings from outdoor-sown vegetables and hardy annuals. Try to find somewhere to replant the strongest discards, for it's a pity to waste them.

Mulch young top fruit and soft fruit with as much well-rotted compost, manure or peat as you can; try to make a layer at least 2in deep in the areas beneath the canopies of trees and shrubs. If you plan to move your spring bulbs, dig them up now and replant them in close lines on your chosen site. Keep them fed and watered so that they'll be in good heart for transplanting in the autumn.

Pruning

On newly established fruit trees, prune away all but six fruit. Remove all but four leaves from vegetative shoots on fan-trained apricots, peaches, nectarines and morello cherries. Thin raspberry suckers to leave four or five good shoots per crown to develop and carry fruit next year; and cut away any strawberry runners not required to establish next year's young plants.

This is a good month to thin and cut back any evergreen shrubs which need reshaping, and you should prune any deciduous shrubs which have finished flowering.

Security

Provide stakes for tall-growing plants such as delphiniums. Be ready for pests. Carrots should be treated against carrot fly, and you should look out for lively hopping flea beetles among the seedlings of every kind of plant. Old-fashioned derris powder controls them very efficiently. Watch out for slug damage and spread slug bait as soon as you see any. Look also for the tell-tale U-shaped holes chewed from the edges of leaves in evergreen shrubs. These are caused by vine weevils, whose grubs do a great deal of damage to roots. Spray both the foliage and the ground with a mixture of permethrin and heptenophos. A spraying with permethrin/heptenophos mixture at petal-fall will also protect apple trees against sawfly. Spray raspberries and other cane fruit with malathion to control raspberry beetles. Treat raspberries at the first pink fruit stage and loganberries both at the end of flowering and 14 days later.

Outdoor planting

Divide and replant spring-flowering plants such as arabis, aubrietia, daisies and primroses. Plant out half-hardy bedding plants, and plants such as scabious and violets which were reared indoors. Hydrangeas and other pot plants taken indoors for the winter can now also be put out in the garden.

Vegetables raised indoors – sprouts, cauliflowers, self-blanching celery, leeks and onions plus outdoor bush tomatoes – should all be planted out this month.

Outdoor sowing

Introduce a little individuality to the garden by sowing a variegated beer hop near a fence, drainpipe or unsightly shed.

Once it's established it will rampage at up to 2ft per day.

Now is the time for sowing sweetcorn (at 18in intervals in rows 18in apart). Wind pollination will be encouraged if you sow in short rows to form rectangular blocks. Rake additional Growmore fertiliser into the soil surface before sowing. In cooler northern counties it pays to sow the seed in 3in pots indoors in mid-april and to wait until June to plant it out. Alternatively, sow outdoors and cover with a cloche.

Wherever you are, you should be sowing more successional crops such as lettuce, radish, beetroot and dwarf beans; plus swedes and kale for the winter. Sow also chervil, parsley, and runner beans. The beans look most attractive if they are sown in threes at the feet of tall canes set at 3ft intervals around a circle and wired together at the top to form a wigwam. When the seedlings have germinated leave only the strongest looking ones to develop.

In the flower garden sow aquilegia, asters, auriculas, Brompton stocks, forget-me-nots, foxgloves, night-scented stocks, gypsophila, polyanthus, primroses and sweet williams.

Feeding

Any spare compost or manure should be laid as a mulch around established fruit trees, which benefit enormously if you treat them this way once every three

Primula auricula – some of the better hybrids have flowers
which are among the smartest in the plant kingdom.
With very bold eye markings their petals appear to
have been painted with the shiniest of enamels. They
look wonderful when massed or grown in wide bands.

years. All soft fruit will benefit from a dose of rose fertiliser applied now.

Lawn work

In periods after rain towards the end of the month, when the lawn is growing well, apply a selective weedkiller to deal with most common weeds. Attack persistent lawn weeds such as woodrush by spot treatments with jelly formulations of glyphosate.

Lawns which have suffered from years of neglect can be rejuvenated by harsh treatment now. Hire a really heavy and powerful scarifier and aerator, and use it thoroughly to drag out all the dead thatch which accumulates at the base of lawn turf. The best kind of aerator has hollow tines set on a roller which remove deep plugs of soil from beneath the sward, allowing the free passage of air, water and fertiliser into the root zone.

On newly sown lawns, unless they look really well established, don't apply weedkiller until September. But do continue topping the developing grass to about 2in and dig out by hand any obvious large weeds like thistles and docks which have not been controlled by mowing.

Maintenance

Now that most of the major cultivation work is complete, it's time to examine your tools. Anything with a split or bro-

ken shaft should be re-handled, and anything metal which is worth repairing should be taken to the blacksmith or garage. Replace anything you found useful but is now too badly broken to be mended, and bear in mind when you buy new tools that it's worth paying extra for increased durability.

In the greenhouse

To avoid plants being scorched in hot weather, spray a temporary shading material on to panes receiving direct sunlight. Keep a constant watch on ventilation and humidity. If conditions are too dry, moisten the air by splashing water on the floor of the house. Make sure that vents are well open from 8 a.m. until sunset on clear days, unless the wind is from the north or east. Continue the whitefly vigil, using permethrin smokes whenever they appear.

Now that the greenhouse is clear of many of the annual plants, take the opportunity to give it a general clean out and tidy. Cut away the stems which have borne flowers on any woody pot plants. Take and set leaf cuttings of African violets or gloxinias, and stem cuttings from houseplants like hibiscus and philodendron.

If you want to produce something exotic in the glasshouse, sow seeds of *Clitoria* 'Double Blue Sails', which produces a great profusion of beautiful deep blue flowers; or the coral tree, which has attractive blue-green foliage and waxy crimson flowers.

Visits

The Mecca for gardeners from all over the world must this month be the Royal Horticultural Society's 'Chelsea Flower Show' in London.

Usually opening to the public on the third Wednesday of the month it offers a unique gardening experience. Its situation alone, in the grounds of Wren's beautiful Royal Hospital (home of the famous red-coated Chelsea Pensioners) on the Thames embankment, justifies the visit.

The best of the new and old varieties of plant are displayed by nurserymen and amateurs under more than four acres of canvas marquee. Elsewhere there are demonstration gardens of all shapes, sizes and styles and the latest equipment for tending gardens of all types from manorial parks to tiny hanging baskets.

The only thing the show really lacks is room for the crowds. More than 300,000 keen gardeners regularly attend the show. And the best time to see it with the least hassle is either very early in the morning or when the worst of the crowds have gone home after 5 in the evening.

NATURAL PEST CONTROL

Gardeners wishing to rid themselves of the two principal glasshouse scourges,

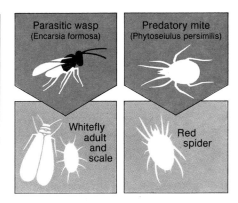

whitefly and red spider, without resorting to pesticides might like to try biological control using parasites instead.

Liberated into the glasshouse when whitefly begin to show their presence, parasitic wasps of the *Encarsia formosa* family will wreak havoc among them. Thrusting their stiletto-like ovipositors into the whiteflies they lay eggs which hatch into minute grubs which kill the whiteflies by eating them away from the inside. The predatory mite *Phytoseilus persimilis* is more overt about the way in which it despatches red spiders. Like a carnivorous commando it savagely gobbles them up and bolts them down.

Both species of parasite and predator are available from Natural Pest Control, Watermead, Yapton Road, Barnham, Bognor Regis, PO22 0BQ.

VERTICAL GARDENS

Few garden features are more attractive than a planted wall. It can be used as a genuine boundary, separating one part of a garden from another. Or it can be regarded simply as a free-standing decorative feature. Building it need not be difficult if you follow these tips.

Construction

Dry walls of irregular quarried stone, or brick walls of 4ft or more in height, are best built by expert craftsmen. Do-it-yourselfers should stick to peat blocks, or to walling slabs. The latter are available as 12in by 8in by 2½in pieces. As their broad surfaces are smooth, low walls of 2ft or less can be laid straight on top of flattened earth, without foundations. Built up one on top of another, they easily produce a stable wall with no need for cement.

Planting

Alpine plants are ideal for growing on walls. It is best to plant them as the wall is being built. Failing this, leave plenty of planting spaces in the face of the wall.

Wall-tops and cavities should be filled with a growing compost of two parts loam (or top-spit soil), one part leaf-mould or fine-grade granulated moss-peat, one part sharp sand. Dust the ingredients generously with bone meal before mixing them together.

If your alpines have been pot-grown, you can plant at any time. But spring or autumn planting reduces the need for watering during the establishment period in summer.

Choosing plants

For the top edges of the wall: *Gypsophila repens* 'Letchworth Rose' – rich pink flowers; *Helianthemum* 'Ben Ledi' – deep wine red and many other colours; Phlox 'Snow Queen' – pure white and many others; *Polygonum vaccinifolium* – heather pink flowers; *Zauschneria californica* 'Mexicana' – scarlet flowers.

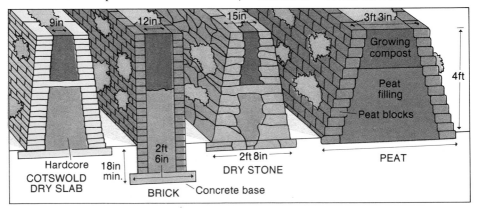

For the crown of the wall: *Anthericum ramosum* – grassy leaves and white flowers: *Aster alpinus* – blue and gold daisies: *Campanula carpatica* – large purple bells: *Geranium* 'Ballerina' – rounded pink flowers: *Potentilla megalantha* – golden flowers, velvety leaves.

For the sunny side of the wall: *Aubretia* 'Belisha Beacon' – bright rose red: *Dianthus arvernensis* – grey mats with pink flowers; *Hypericum olympicum* – low bushes and gold flowers; *Saxifraga* 'Esther' – soft yellow flowers.

For the shady side of the wall: *Chiastophyllum oppositifolium* – dangling chains of yellow flowers; *Mentha requienii* – lavender flowers; *Saxifraga moschata* 'Cloth of Gold' – dense tufts of golden leaves, white flowers.

PLANTS OF THE MONTH

TREES

Sorbus aria 'Lutescens' – cream flowers and felted leaves.

Cornus florida 'White Cloud' – white petal-like bracts.

SHRUBS

Embothrium lanceolatum – orange scarlet flowers.

Tamarisk tetrandra – light pink flowers.

Olearia x scilloniensis – white daisies.

Ceanothus arboreus – 'Trewithen Blue' – deep blue flowers.

BORDER PLANTS

Anemone lesseri – a dwarf with rose carmine flowers.

Astrantia major – pinkish green flowers.

Euphorbia griffithii 'Fire Glow' – vivid pink red flowers.

Iris 'Mary McIlroy' – a miniature with yellow blooms.

Primula auricula – shiny petals.

Sisyrinchium brachypus – buttercup yellow flowers.

June

After the spring rush, gardeners can work at a more leisurely pace for the following few months. There is no point in having a garden if you don't have time to enjoy it. This is the time, too, when the success of the previous year's efforts can be appraised. Half close your eyes and try to look at the garden from many angles. Try to probe its weaknesses in form or colour harmony. Imagine how it would look if you widened or eliminated paths, re-shaped beds, raised or lowered the level of the ground, replaced grass by paving or terracing, and positioned figures or other artefacts in strategic places to beckon the eye or distract attention.

Allow your mind to stray from plantsmanship and husbandry to picture-making and landscape architecture and note down your observations so you can instigate your transformations during autumn and winter.

Ground and water work

Draw soil up round early leeks to start blanching them, and pull the soil away from the base of shallots to ripen the cloves. Hold weeds in check, and keep the soil surface loose by hoeing among vegetable crops and in flower beds and shrubberies. Provided rain isn't forecast, you can leave weed seedlings to wilt away. Continue to draw soil from the furrows to earth-up developing maincrop potatoes.

Finish cutting asparagus on the twentieth of the month, then run strings on canes around the bed to support the developing fern, which must be allowed to flourish to feed the crowns for next year's crop.

Never let the ground carrying vegetable and salad crops dry out completely. A thick mulch of lawn clippings above the roots of such crops as runner beans will help keep the soil moist.

Test dig early potatoes at the end of the month. If they are ready, lift only one plant at a time, digging more as required. Keep the area tidy by putting discarded stems and foliage on to the compost heap. If they are grown under black plastic, cut it away little by little and dump it straight into the garbage – nothing looks worse than shrubs festooned with plastic.

Lift and split overlarge clumps of aquatic plants in the pond early in the month: and now that the vegetable patch is set and growing well, lay down any portable irrigation piping which you plan to use during the hot months.

Pruning

Thin out crowded rows of all plants to their final growing distances. Continue to remove side shoots from indoor tomatoes. Dead-head anything which has finished flowering – unless it has attractive seed pods – and cut back fairly hard many alpines which have flowered to encourage vigorous regrowth.

Thin autumn-fruiting raspberries to leave six or seven vigorous stems. After apple trees have shed some of their fruit naturally, remove any remaining diseased or malformed fruit: try to leave apples at about six-inch intervals. Early in the month plums can be thinned so that none of them are so close as to restrict the growth of their neighbours.

Cut out any signs of silver leaf disease on plums, peaches or cherries; cut back until brown stains inside the branches are no longer evident.

Prune away unwanted shoots developing on fan-trained pears, plums and cherries.

Prune roses as their flowers begin to fade, and cut back to the base of flower stems. Pick off faded blooms from rhododendrons and azaleas; and cut away lilac suckers with a sharp knife well below soil level.

Security

Caterpillars are the main scourge in June. Keep looking out for them after the butterflies have appeared and spray to control; old-fashioned derris sprays are effective.

Broad beans are likely to be attacked by blackfly. Snap off their soft growing points where the blackfly first congregate; if the attack continues, spray with a systemic insecticide. Both a soil insecticide and a contact spray based on permethrin will be necessary if pea and bean weevils start to bite notches in the leaves of these crops. Their larvae also feed on the roots.

If there has been a spell of warm, damp weather, potatoes could be attacked by potato blight late in the month. A good protection can be obtained by spraying with a liquid copper fungicide and repeating the treatment twice more at fourteen day intervals.

Including a permethrin/heptenophos mixture in the routine fungicidal spray in mid-month should prevent apples from becoming maggoty due to codding moth; this treatment should be repeated twice at twenty-one day intervals.

Spray with the same insecticide to control aphids, capsids and sawfly on plums or other stone fruit and on black, red or white currants and gooseberries. Use a systemic fungicide to control gooseberry mildew and leaf spot diseases.

Tie up all climbers to their supporting wires to prevent their developing stems

'Mary Rose' – one of the best of the 'new' old-type roses bred by David Austin. It has the attractive blooms and fragrance, hardiness and disease resistance of the old shrub roses combined with the repeat flowering ability of modern hybrids

being snapped in wind, and stack and tie up tall plants like carnations.

To prevent seeding, snap off the stems of autumn-sown onions as soon as flower heads are seen.

Outdoor planting

Plant leeks and transplant winter brassicas to their final places, puddling them well in with water. Fuchsias, salvias, zinnias, cannas and begonias, either bought at the nursery or home grown, should be put out this month, too.

Divide and replant irises, and make a little nursery bed in a corner of the garden and plant cuttings of sweet william to produce good plants for next year.

Plant container-grown shrubs and trees – and be sure to keep them well watered.

Tease out the growing point of pinks and stick them into a layer of grit over topsoil to form new plants.

Outdoor sowing

Fast-growing annuals, like alyssum and virginia stocks, can be sown to fill unexpected gaps in borders. Sow biennials, like sweet william, Canterbury bell, foxglove and forget-me-not, in places where you want them in the border next year, and thin after germination. Wallflowers, primroses, polyanthus, pansies and violas can also be treated in this way. If there is no room in the beds, raise them in boxes for transplanting in autumn.

Sprinkle seeds of *Erinus alpinus* over the rockery or planted walls. This evergreen, hardy perennial will fill gaps and give the area a very natural look.

Try some ambitious sowing of brooms in boxes; move them into three-inch pots as soon as they are large enough to handle and plant them out this autumn.

Continue sequential sowing of salad crops, and make a final sowing of shorthorn carrots. Sow cucumbers on well-fed outdoor beds, and sow maincrop turnips.

Feeding

Include liquid feed when watering tomatoes, cucumbers, courgettes and squashes. Water strawberries copiously, including liquid fertiliser, and be generous with plants whose runners have been pegged down to root and form new plants for next year.

Lawn work

Give the lawn an occasional thorough soaking at night during long, dry spells. Spray with a liquid fertiliser and water well. Mow with the box off in really hot weather.

In the greenhouse

From now on be generous with liquid fertiliser on tomatoes, cucumbers, courgettes and squashes.

Take four-inch, semi-hard wood cuttings from shrubs such as camellia, cistus, ceanothus, viburnum, pyracanthas, escallonia, eleagnus and potentilla. Cut them from young branches whose bark has begun to ripen. Dip their bases in rooting hormone and stick their bottom two inches into pots containing a 50-50 mixture of peat and coarse sand. Water well and encase pots in closed polythene bags to conserve moisture.

Continue to watch for the appearance of whitefly and fumigate if necessary.

Visits

Traditionally the month when roses are at their peak, local gardens with a reputation for them should obviously be included in gardeners' weekend itineraries during June. But this is also the month when rose fetishists should climb into their cars and speed away to St Albans to see for themselves the glory of the display in the gardens of the Royal National Rose Society.

Apart from an astonishing array of new varieties – many of them still on trial and unnamed – the older and frequently more attractive varieties from which they were bred compete well for attention.

As you would expect, all the roses at St Albans are superbly grown; this allows visitors to realise what their own plants could become if they are looked after well. It is also interesting to see concentrated in a single specialist garden the host of ways in which roses can be grown – in containers, against walls, along ropes and chains etc.

THE ALPINE GARDEN

There always seems to be some corner of a garden which demands something exquisite. And a well-made bed of good

The well-made rockery is a good home for alpine plants. The rockery pavement (1) at the foot of large key stones (2) form the basis of the rockery holding back the earth supporting mound-making plants (3). Erect plants (4) at the foot of each stratum of rock can be interspersed with rosette-forming plants in the cracks (5). Creeping plants look lovely spilling over the rocks (6) and screes of gravel and small stones (7)

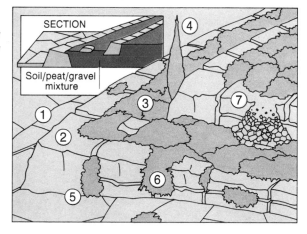

rock and gravel as a home for alpine plants often supplies that need.

The basis of an alpine garden is a series of rock walls forming shallow obtuse angles (see illustration). The space behind each wall is packed with a 50-50 mixture of heavy loam and ¼in gravel chippings (for drainage). Each walled terrace forms a foundation for the one above it, and a minimum of three levels is needed to achieve the right effect.

The rocks in the walls are arranged in parallel 'strata', sloping towards the soil behind the terrace to give an impression of natural outcrops, which is further enhanced by careful planting.

Small evergreen conifers are placed behind the terraces to make an ideal backdrop; and the larger rock-faces themselves are made more intriguing by being glimpsed through the foliage of miniature conifers and other erect shrubs and herbaceous plants. Rosette-forming plants cling to the crannies between the rocks, while carpet-formers spread across them and hang down. The gentler terrace slopes and the steeper parts of the 'screes' (where gravel and small rocks spill from one terrace to another) are clad with literally hundreds of varieties of small-leaved alpine plants, forming tightly compacted mounds like pincushions and carrying a seasonal fuzz of tiny brilliant flowers.

The choice of plants must obviously depend to some extent on whether the basic soil is acid or alkaline. But there are many dwarf shrubs and flowering plants that will provide colour in all seasons and in all soils – literally hundreds of beautiful members of the saxifrage, primula, campanula, androsace, gentian and phlox families, for example. Fine tussocky mountain fescue grass (which never needs mowing) can also be used to cover patches of terrace, and will spread to fill the larger cracks in the rock.

BREEDING A ROSE . . .

No gardener should die without once having tried to breed a rose of their very own. And it isn't difficult because most floribundas and hybrid teas will readily interbreed.

Buy two likely container-grown plants at the garden centre which are showing plenty of bud. Try a white and a red in the hope that some of the progeny will have attractive pink petals. They will have to be kept indoors so you must keep them well fed and watered.

Ripe pollen from the male parent is best obtained when the flower is fully open. Close examination with a hand-lens will reveal the pollen as a yellow powder thickly coating the anthers at the tips of the stamens. Remove the stamens entirely, using a pair of fine pointed tweezers. They will then remain fresh for several days inside a small closed, transparent plastic box – provided they are kept cool and dry and free from contamination by tiny pieces of torn petal or other plant debris.

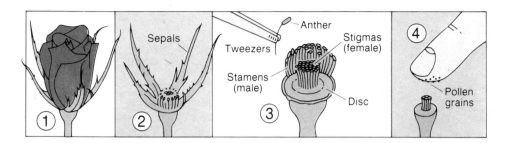

Then timing is the really crucial factor. The stigmas of the female parent must be receptive but you have to catch them before they have been naturally pollinated. Do that by examining the developing flower buds at eight o'clock each morning. Loosen the ones which are likely to begin opening that day (the fattest ones, already showing their petal-colour). With tweezers strip the sepals, petals and stamens from each of these buds, leaving only the exposed central stigmas. Then dip the tip of a finger into the plastic box of stamens and sprinkle a light dusting of pollen over all the stigma heads. Then enclose each bud in a small paper bag, fitting like a loose mitten and fastened to the stem with twine.

The process of fertilisation takes between five and seven days, and the bag should not be removed until the light-coloured disc around the stigmas has darkened.

Flower buds pollinated in this way will develop into normal hips, and the gardener has nothing further to do until they are fully ripe in November. The hips then should be gently broken open so that the pips – or more correctly, achenes – containing the seeds can be scooped out without damage. Each hip will contain anything from one to forty viable seeds capable of growing into plants of a new variety.

They are sown at ½in intervals, just below the surface of seed compost, in a plastic seed pan labelled with details of the parents. Kept just moist in a cool airy place, and protected from frost and mice, most of the seeds should have germinated by the end of February. In late March or early April, once they have developed two pairs of true leaves (and provided they have shown no obvious faults), they should be transferred to 3½in pots containing John Innes No. 2 compost. If kept in a glasshouse, the seedlings should form their first tiny flower buds when they are about 3in high.

PLANTS OF THE MONTH

TREES

Laburnum alpinum – the best of the laburnums.

Liriodendron tulipifera aureo marginatum – with variegated leaves and greenish yellow flowers with orange centres.

SHRUBS

Buddleia globosa – orange globe flowers.

Genista hispanica – golden broom flowers.

Phlomis fruticosa – smoky yellow flowers.

Leptospermum scorparium 'Red Damask' – double red flowers.

BORDER PLANTS

Lilium pumilum – scarlet Turk's cap flowers.

Hosta tardiana – a dwarf variety with lavender flowers.

Hemerocallis 'Contessa' – bright orange flowers.

Gladiolus nanus 'Prince Claus' – white petals with red blotches.

Alchemilla erythropoda – bluish foliage and sulphur flowers.

July

If we are lucky, summer will begin to hang a warm mantle over the garden this month and we'll need to finish the modicum of essential heavy work before the sun is high and has evaporated our resolution. Wisely we will wait until the shadows lengthen before taking the watering can or hose to refresh parched plants in baked earth.

Ah well, we can always dream! Should these golden expectations remain unfulfilled, we can reflect in consolation that no amount of water applied through can or hose will do as much good as a heavy shower of rain.

Ground work

Much of the effort in early morning or late evening will be devoted to hoeing gently along the vegetable rows and among the flower beds to cut out weeds and loosen the soil to let the air and water in. Don't hoe too deeply close to shallow-rooted plants, or you will do more harm than good. Now is the time to pull away loose soil from the base of shallots and give the potatoes a final earthing up.

Pruning

The aim here is to trim away unnecessary summer growth, particularly if it is shading fruit, and to thin fruit on overcrowded branches. It's also a good month to remove unwanted shoots from fruit trees like figs, apricots, plums and cherries which are being trained against walls; and to prune evergreen hedges, giving the new shoots time to ripen properly before the winter frosts.

To ensure recurrent flowering, roses should be dead-headed as soon as each bloom begins to drop its petals. Many of the early- and mid-season plants in the herbaceous borders will have finished flowering and should be cut back hard to stimulate bushy new growth for next year. If you want large chrysanthemums, now is the time to pinch out the lateral flower buds.

Security

Leaf vegetables in particular loathe droughts, and need water each evening in hot dry weather. Tomatoes, too, become very niggardly if left to swelter without relief, and new lawns and newly-planted trees and shrubs must be given special attention if they are not to suffer – sometimes fatally – from lack of water.

Powdery mildews luxuriate in dry weather; downy mildews in the steamy conditions after rain has fallen on warm ground. Heat stimulates the metabolism of insects, causing them to multiply like freckles in the sun – a frenzy they can support only by gobbling up your plants. So keep your sprayer at the ready, and try to choose products which are not only effective but also safe for family and pets, doing their work quickly and then disappearing to cause the least amount of ecological upset. More and more of the larger pesticide producers have yielded to pressure and are now producing formulations of this type.

Tall-growing border plants in exposed positions should be staked to prevent them collapsing in wind. Lawn weedkillers should be applied when the grass is growing well after rain. You won't get another good chance to attack lawn weeds until the autumn.

Outdoor planting

Dig up and replant iris rhizomes, and finish planting out any seedlings you sowed earlier in the year. Biennials and perennials should be moved to their final homes in the flower beds. Plant out kale, broccoli and celery in the vegetable garden where crops of peas, beans and spring cabbage have been removed. Although it is more usual to split up and move perennial herbaceous plants in the autumn, if space for replanting is available now, this is not a bad time to move some of the earlier flowering varieties. If you do, you will have to water them well during dry weather.

Outdoor sowing

Sow seed of perennial and biennial flowers for flowering next year. It's always a good idea to have plenty of pansies ready, so sow a few packets of seed on compost in boxes outdoors.

Endive can be sown in a half shaded area of the vegetable garden, and it is also a good time to sow more lettuce, radishes and turnips for eating later in the year.

Feeding

After the spring growth-burst, many plants will have depleted the readily available nutrients in the soil. A light top dressing of fertiliser around the bases of trees and shrubs, or between growing crops, can now be very beneficial.

Include liquid feed when watering tomatoes and sweet peas. Mulch dahlias with manure or well-rotted compost.

If shrubs or border plants are obviously running out of nutrients, spray the leaves with a foliar feed.

Lawn work

Apart from some weedkilling if the weather is right (see above) the best advice this month is to raise the cutter blades by half an inch. Shallow-rooted lawn grasses suffer badly in dry spells and removing too much top over-exposes the soil surface to evaporation and only makes matters worse.

Romneya coulteri – this giant among the poppy
family can tower up to 8ft and established
clumps can dominate large borders like
gracious duchesses.

Maintenance

There are few better disinfectants than hot sunshine. When a day promises to be bright, scrub out all the used pots and boxes and allow them to dry out thoroughly before stacking them away.

In the greenhouse

This is a good time to take cuttings of many shrubs and get them firmly rooted in the warmth of the greenhouse. Sink several at a time deeply in very damp gritty compost in pots, or individually in trays of small square pots after dipping their ends in rooting hormone. Seal the pots in a polythene bag or the trays under a rigid polythene cover to keep the compost permanently damp. Cuttings of rock plants and pinks can also be rooted in the glasshouse now.

Copious watering will be necessary this month for all plants growing in the greenhouse, and it usually pays to leave the ventilators open all night. Climbing plants need a lot of tying in as they respond to summer temperatures by making rapid fragile growth. The value of automating both watering and ventilation in the greenhouse becomes really evident when hot weather and drying winds coupled with vigorous growth can impose serious stress on the plants. Ventilation control is easily achieved by means of a small device which attaches to the bottom of the vent and its surrounding frame. In essence it is a small cylinder filled with wax. The volume of the wax changes as the temperature goes up and down, thus moving a piston within the cylinder which in turn operates a lever attached to the piston rod. You can adjust the length of the lever to ensure that the vent is fully opened during very hot periods, or fully closed when the temperature falls dangerously at night.

Several kinds of automatic watering systems are now available to amateur greenhouse growers. In some of them the containerised plants stand on capillary matting which draws water from a trough. As the water level in the trough reduces, it is replenished from a cistern via a floating control-valve. In other systems, water direct from the mains is fed down standard hose and then through small-bore plastic tubing to drip-emitters. These can be positioned to slowly irrigate plants either in pots or growing in the ground. Output can be tailored to meet the needs of particular plants, varying from nothing to approximately two gallons per hour.

Seeds of pinks and Brompton stocks or spring-flowering calceolarias can be sown now, and cinerarias sown earlier should be ready for pricking out. Tender rhododendrons and azaleas can now safely stand outdoors; cyclamen and primulas should be moved into their flowering pots and anything which has become rootbound should be repotted.

Visits

This is the month for seeking out the gardens with the long and deep herbaceous borders which should be at the height of their summer glory.

Although fewer and fewer great gardens can afford the labour – or amateur gardeners the time – to produce the riots of colour which astonished our grandparents, it is herbaceous borders at their best which still provoke the loudest gasps of pleasure among garden visitors. That is why few great gardens open to the public don't make some attempt at herbaceous gardens even if on a reduced scale.

Gardens like Barrington Court, near Ilminster in Somerset; Pusey House, near Faringdon, Oxfordshire; Hidcote Manor, Mickleton, Gloucestershire; Great Dixter, Etchingham, East Sussex; Arley Hall, nr. Warrington, Cheshire; Newby Hall, Boroughbridge, Yorkshire; and Leith Hall, Kennethmont, Grampian are all still proud of their borders.

SUCCESSFUL CUTTINGS

If you want the satisfaction of multiplying your most beautiful trees and shrubs to be able to enrich your garden and that of friends at little cost, now is the time to root the cuttings.

Always take summer cuttings from the soft to medium-hard twigs at the end of this season's growth. Using secateurs, cut off 6 to 8in of tip growth depending upon

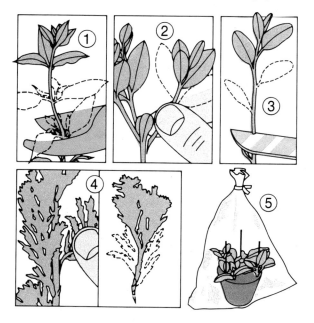

the vigour of the plant; for ericas (heathers) take only 2in.

The way cuttings for planting are produced from the cutting material depends upon the variety of tree or shrub.

Fuchsias (drawing 1), philadelphus, buddleia, cistus, deutzia, which have paired leaves should have 2 to 3in sections cut from the cutting material. The two lower pairs of leaves should be snipped off close to the stem.

Azaleas (drawing 2), ericas, escallonias, cytisus, pyracantha and cotoneaster, which have leaves occuring alternately on the stem, should have an individual shoot of about 2 to 3in torn from the stem between the thumb and forefinger by pulling gently downwards. The ragged heel where the shoot has broken away from the stem should be trimmed with secateurs or scissors and the leaves from the bottom 1 to 1½in should then be trimmed away.

Other shrubs with alternate leaves like senecio (drawing 3), vinca, spirea or pachysandra should only be cut into 2 to 4in lengths, cutting just below a leaf and removing the lower two leaves.

Conifers (drawing 4) like *Juniperus tamariskifolia, Chamaecyparis lawsonianaellwoodii, Cupressocyparis leylandii* or the thujas, should have their 2 to 4in individual fronds torn away from the shoot then the heel trimmed and the lower inch of leaflets removed with a knife, secateurs or sharp thumbnail.

Trimmed cuttings should be planted in a moist mixture of half peat and half coarse sand. Dip the bottom ½in of cutting in a hormone rooting compound containing a fungicide to prevent rotting. Short cuttings like ericas should be pressed ½ to ¾in into the mixture and longer cuttings to a depth of 1 to 1½in. Space the short cuttings ¾in apart and the larger cuttings 1 to 1½in.

Any container giving a minimum depth of 2in of mixture will do. A standard seedbox or a 6in pot are best. Once planted, the cuttings should be very thoroughly watered and allowed to drain. No further water should be necessary until the cuttings have rooted, provided that the pot or container is completely sealed into a transparent plastic bag using flexible twist ties. This sealed environment prevents evaporation and keeps the growing medium and cuttings moist. To prevent the top of the bag collapsing on to the cuttings, put three small canes in the compost to provide support (drawing 5).

Place the sealed containers in a glasshouse, porch, garden frame, or on a window ledge in a position where they can be protected from direct sunlight. A sheet of newspaper makes good shade. It is important to ensure that in very bright weather the cuttings do not become scorched.

When it is obvious the cuttings are beginning to grow (usually after about two months) open the top of the bag to admit more air gradually. After a few days remove the bag completely. At this stage the rooted cuttings must be potted. Use a proprietary potting compost and establish the ericas in approximately 2in diameter pots and the large cuttings in 3 to 3½in pots. Put the newly potted young plants in a protected environment for the winter and make sure that they never dry out.

THE SILVER SIX

There is a fascination about the notion of creating a monochromatic garden in which only subtle changes in tone and the differences in the form and texture of plants provide the interest. Among the most attractive borders are those in which silver (or at least a silvery green) is the predominant colour. And their advantage over other single colour borders is that so many of the silver plants are evergreen and look well right through the winter. Six of the most interesting are:

1. *Tanacetum densum-amanum.* This provides a quick growing woolly rug which covers the ground and throws up tiny heads like Prince of Wales feathers.
2. *Digitalis heywoodii.* This is the Spanish foxglove. It has spectacular white-edged leaves, spires of pinky white flowers and grows to 2½ft.
3. *Helichrysum angustifolium* has silver leaves. An alternative, *Helichrysum fontanesii*, has felty white leaves. Both grow to 3ft.

4. *Verbascum* 'Frosty Gold'. As verbascums go this is a mini-variety only 3ft tall. It has furry leaves and its spires carry primrose-yellow flowers.
5. *Artemisia arborescens.* A spectacular silver sparkler which grows to 4ft.
6. *Senecio* 'Ramparts'. Forms huge snowballs; grows to 4½ft. Alternative variety is White Diamond.

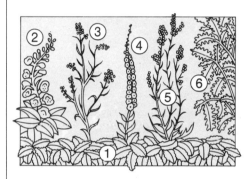

PLANTS OF THE MONTH

TREES

Cornus macrophylla – large leaves with creamy white flowers and blue-black fruit.

Eucryphia glutinosa – white flowers with conspicuous stamens.

SHRUBS

Indigofera gerardiana – purple pea-blue flowers.

Teucrium fruticans – pale blue flowers.

Hoheria glabrata – fragrant translucent white flowers.

Fuchsia 'Riccartonii' – scarlet flowers.

BORDER PLANTS

Allium flavum – golden yellow flowers.

Astilbe sinensis pumila – lilac pink flowers.

Crocosmia 'Emberglow' – deep orange flowers.

Lilium 'Green Dragon' – white and green trumpets.

Helianthemum 'Red Orient' – a single red daisy.

August

This is the month when you wake up on your holiday beach and start to worry about what's going on at home. Will the neighbour remember her promise to pop in every evening and give a quick squirt with the hose? Will the automatic irrigation system function properly? Frenzied speculations like these have driven many gardeners home days early from their holidays – and of course the only way to avoid such anxieties is to do all you can to leave things in better order before you leave home.

Hoe out or spot-spray any weed seedlings developing on planted areas. Plenty more will emerge during your absence, but with luck they won't have time to compete too fiercely with the cultivated plants. Ensure that the watering devices function really efficiently – particularly those fitted with automatic valves governed by soil moisture sensors.

Leave any seed-sowing until you get back so that you can be there to control conditions during the crucial germination period. Don't be tempted to get things going before you leave in the hope that on your return you will be 'a step ahead'.

Ground work

Thunder showers this month can compact soil and cause it to dry like concrete. Break through the crust with a border fork. Since it is likely that there will be more warm dry weather to come, use any compost which has built up and matured during the season to mulch over the roots of shrubs – particularly moisture-lovers like rhododendrons. Earth up celery and leeks.

Pruning

Continue the summer pruning of fruit trees. The fruits of apricots, peaches and nectarines should be quite unshaded by foliage if they are to ripen well. Cut out the canes of summer-fruiting raspberries and loganberries which have borne fruit. Remove all unwanted runners from strawberries. Cut back the stalks of artichokes once their heads have been gathered. Take off the seed heads put up by asparagus crowns. Remove dead flower spikes from antirrhinums, leaving an odd one to throw seed and provide nice surprises next year. This is the best time to trim lavender hedges: they take a long time to recover if cut back hard in the winter.

Security

Pests and diseases will continue to prosper in the warm weather, so be on your guard. Protect wall fruit from wasps and

birds as it ripens. Fine nets will ward off the birds; small greaseproof paper bags fastened round individual fruits will keep off the wasps. If you can't find made-up bags, the paper is still available in sheets and you can turn it into bags using the office stapler. Trap earwigs with a damp washing-up cloth, in which they will hide during the day, and lure slugs with grape-fruit skins or beer.

Outdoor planting

Plant narcissus bulbs now to ensure a good show next spring. It is also a good time to plant amaryllis, colchicum, cyclamen, Guernsey lilies and well-struck cuttings of pinks. Seedlings of perennials can be transplanted to their permanent sites, and spring-flowering perennials divided and replanted. Plant cuttings of hardy geraniums and the offsets of saxifrages.

New strawberry beds can be created by planting well-rooted runners from the old ones. Broccoli, cabbages, celery and endive can also be planted out now.

Outdoor sowing

Sow annuals for flowering next spring, especially antirrhinums, pansies, Iceland poppies and violas. Sow 'intermediate' stocks early in the month and 'ten-week stocks' two weeks later in boxes outdoors. They can then be potted on and taken into the greenhouse before the first frost. Sow cauliflowers, corn salad, lettuce, onions, red cabbage, spinach and turnips.

Feeding

Continue to give sweet peas and tomatoes plenty of water supplemented with a high potash liquid feed throughout the month. They both do best if the top soil is never allowed to dry out.

In the greenhouse

Make sure greenhouse plants standing out of doors are given a good wetting spray with water every evening. Late-flowering azaleas should be repotted. Climbing plants should be cut back to keep them within bounds. Lilies which

have flowered need less water. Annuals for winter flowering can be sown now; so too can cyclamens, geraniums, pelargoniums and schizanthus.

Cuttings of arabis, many hardy rock plants, fuchsias, geraniums, heliotrope, hydrangeas and other half-hardy plants can be struck this month.

Calceolarias and cinerarias can be potted off from seed boxes when they are robust enough to stand the move. Primulas should be divided and planted into 5in pots. If you'd like to introduce some novelty to your garden, three plants worth sowing in the greenhouse are the migno-

Abutilon megapotanicum – is the perfect climber for a low wall in a protected sunny place. It will quickly reach 8 ft and produce charming yellow bells with crimson calyxes and it continues flowering for a long period.

nette 'Fragrant Beauty', the balloon flower and the blue lace flower.

The mignonette produces charming scented flowers and makes a fine spring display when pricked out at three to a 5in pot. Leave them in a cold frame until November, then bring them back into the greenhouse. Balloon flowers sown in boxes in the greenhouse now should be thinned to 6in and then planted out 12in apart in March; by July they will have grown to 18in and carry large blue flowers. Their balloon-like buds can be popped open. Blue lace flowers sown now will produce soft blue scabious-like blooms on 18in tall plants in December and January. Prick them out into 5in pots as soon as they are strong enough to handle.

Don't forget

If you want really large apples and pears you will have to thin them so that there is no more than one fruit left to ripen for every 4in of branch. Plums are best ripened off in a semi-dark store.

Visits

In the heat of August even the best of gardens die a little as they lapse into summer dormancy. And it's a relief on such sultry days to contemplate the reflections in water. That's why water gardens make such a satisfying inclusion in any holidaying gardener's tour programme.

Among others which are worth visiting are Harlow Car, near Harrogate, West Yorkshire; the RHS Gardens at Wisley in Surrey; Barnaby Hall at Pocklington, Humberside; Hodnet Hall, Hodnet, Shropshire; Buscot Park, Buscot, Berkshire; Achamore House, Isle of Ghia, Strathclyde; Westbury Court, Westbury on Severn, Gloucestershire; Chatsworth, Matlock, Derbyshire.

SUPPORTING CLIMBERS

There is no better way of supporting the elongating shoots of non-clinging climbers on walls than to create a framework of ex-army field telephone wire to which they can be easily attached with plastic 'filis'. The wire is really wonderful stuff with a spun copper core and a woven linen cladding, damp-proofed with wax. A truly tough interior with a soft jacket

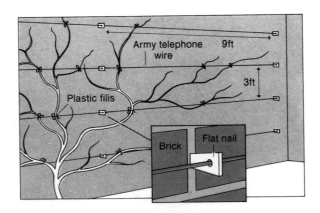

which leaves tender stems wound round it and tugged by the wind completely unbruised. I support the wire on brick walls (see diagram) along lines of cadmium-plated flat 'nails' hammered well into the mortar at intervals of 9 feet. The wire is passed through the holes drilled for it in the tops of the nails and tied at both ends.

Ideally parallel horizontal lines of wire support should be provided at 18in intervals. But to save wire and work I leave 3ft gaps. I make up the deficiency by tying vertical strands of weather-proofed soft twine between the wires when necessary.

A BASIC BORDER

Drab areas in flower beds in August remind us that our gardens would have fewer dead periods if more care was taken in the selection of our border plants. In the following list of herbaceous plants at least three should be in full flower at any one time from May until the end of summer. The numbers correspond to those in the suggested planting plan:

1. *Chrysanthemum maximum* 'Wirral Supreme': white daisy-like flowers on 3ft stems; July to August.
2. *Sidalcea* 'Croftway Red': rich red 3ft spikes of flowers; July to August.
3. *Hemerocallis* 'Burning Daylight': orange, lily-like flowers, June to August; grows to 33in.
4. *Polygonum bistorta superbum*: 3ft light pink pokers; May to August.
5. *Monarda* 'Cambridge Scarlet': round-headed scarlet blossoms 3ft above ground; fragrant foliage; July to September.
6. *Solidago goldenmosa*: at 27in a more compact version of golden rod; August to September.
7. *Liatris callilepis*: 3ft lilac-coloured drumstick flowers; July to September.
8. *Sedum* 'Autumn Joy': juicy grey-green leaves send up 2ft stems headed by discs of tightly packed, rose coloured florets in August which turn dark red in October.
9. *Rudbeckia newmannii*: splendid, black-eyed yellow daisies shoot up to 2ft; July to September.
10. *Salvia superba* 'Lubeca': 30in violet

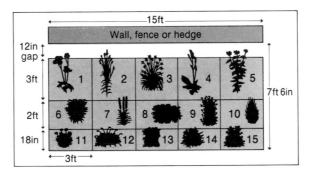

purple spikes; June to September.

11. *Geranium* 'Johnson's Blue': hardy geranium with finely serrated leaves; delicate bright blue flowers on 18in stalks; May to August.

12. *Dicentra eximea* 'Adrian Bloom': delicate fern-like leaves are rich green foil for the dark crimson heart-shaped flowers on 15in stalks; May to July.

13. *Coreopsis verticillata* 'Grandiflora': neat 2ft bushes which carry masses of small yellow flowers; July to September.

14. *Tradescantia virginiana* 'Purple Dome': dark purple rosettes top this 2ft rush-like plant; June to September.

15. *Erigeron* 'Forresters Liebling': semi-double, daisy-like, deep pink flowers on 20in stalks; June to August.

PLANTS OF THE MONTH

TREES

Ligustrum lucidum 'Latifolium' – white flowers.

Koelreuteria paniculata – yellow flowers.

SHRUBS

Hibiscus syriacus 'Blue Bird' – violet blue dark-eyed flowers.

Abelia chinensis 'Francis Mason' – golden variegated foliage and pink flushed white flowers.

Itea ilicifolia – greenish white catkin flowers.

Rubus almifolius bellidiflorus – rose pink flowers.

BORDER PLANTS

Agapanthus 'Headbourne Blue' – mid-blue flowers.

Dierama pumila – salmon pink flowers.

Galtonia viridiflora – lime green flowers.

Lilium tigrinum splendens – black spotted orange Turk's cap flowers.

Tritonia rosea – pink bellflowers.

September

As the air grows increasingly chill, a host of autumn tasks become urgent if you are to get the full benefit of next spring's garden. Act now – the season of mists and mellow forgetfulness will soon be upon us.

Ground work

Areas which have lain fallow because they were dug too late for sowing grass seed or laying turf last spring need to be cleared with a non-persistent contact weedkiller, then forked over. Later in the month they will need raking flat, treading to compact the soil and then raking again to form a seed bed. Lift maincrop potatoes and store them in a bag (sacking or paper, not plastic) in a cool, dry and dark well-ventilated place. Collect and compost all green trash from the vegetable patch. Dig over all areas of the vegetable plot which are free of crops, leaving the surface quite rough. Incorporate as much manure or well-rotted compost as possible into the top soil by scattering it along the digging trench and turning the soil from the next digging line on to it.

Remove fading annuals from the beds and prepare small areas for receiving hardy annual seeds by cultivating them with a border fork. Dig holes to take containerised trees, breaking up the bottom soil to improve drainage and stirring in manure, peat or compost with a fork. Then cover the organic matter with a couple of inches of good top soil. Prepare an area of the vegetable plot to take winter cabbage. More rain during this month usually means more weeds so keep spudding them out with a hoe. Pick them up and dump them on the compost heap or they may reroot in wet weather. Bend down the necks of maturing onion plants to stop them growing and help them to begin drying out.

Pruning

Cut back and tie in the shoots of climbing plants. Disbud the lateral flower buds and thin the shoots of dahlias if you want large blooms. Cut back straggling rock plants so that new shoots are encouraged to break from their crowns. As hollyhocks finish blooming remove their tall flowering stems to leave good compact plants about 18in high. Remove all leaves shading the fruit of tomatoes and thin them to allow the remainder to ripen properly. Continue to prune away unnecessary shoots on wall-trained fruit trees. Also remove all young shoots on pear trees. Remove any shoots developing inside the canopy of cherry trees or any branches which are beginning to cross and rub in the wind. Remove the ends and thin the shoots of gooseberries. Leave only four new growths on raspberries and tie in the canes to the wire. Remove all superfluous strawberry runners and use them for planting elsewhere if you have room. Prune away side sprays from currants.

Security

September can be a very blowy month so stake and tie up everything which could be broken off by gales. Trap earwigs which love dahlias.

Cleaning and tidying

Towards the end of the month many of the later flowering perennials will be past their best and a lot of dead-heading and removing damaged foliage will be required.

Outdoor planting

Finish planting narcissi and such bulbs as crocuses, montbretia, scillas and snowdrops. It's also a good time to plant hardy lilies and irises. Begin transplanting young herbaceous plants from cuttings taken early in the year. Pansy seedlings and offsets of polyanthus and auriculas should also go out now. Cabbages, savoys, spinach, spring greens and lettuce can also be planted out now. The lettuce will fare better if given the protection of a cloche. Although they can be transplanted at any time, September is the perfect month for settling in container-grown shrubs. The soil is still warm which encourages them to develop plenty of new root before winter. And they won't suffer the water stress of shrubs planted earlier.

Outdoor sowing

Sow hardy annuals in the flower garden now. Take a risk on sowing a few antirrhinum – they may survive in a sheltered spot to flower early. Sow a row or two of sweet peas to mask a fence and provide flowers for the house next year. They love moisture so dig a deep trench and pack it with organic matter and then sow the seeds on a layer of topsoil above. Sow a row of lettuce for winter cropping under a cloche.

Lawn work

Increase the height of the mower cutter and after mowing give the lawn a good scrape over with a wire rake. Carry off the rubbish collected. Sow new lawns towards the end of the month after there has been a decent shower. Lawn turf can be laid any time between now and April. But the grass will root into the soil below and the divisions between the turfs will disappear more quickly if it is done now.

The autumn is really the best time to

Anemone japonica – enjoying both full sun or
partial shade it is one of the most elegant of
garden plants. Their flower stems reach 20
inches in height which makes them ideal
subjects for the middle of a border.

lay the instant roll-up lawns sown on plastic mesh which are offered in many areas. But it is worth noting that to be really satisfactory this type of turf needs to be laid on a very level and firm soil base. If possible the level soil should be rolled after being compressed by tramping. This procedure will reveal more hollows than you believed existed and they should be filled with loose soil and further tramping before the turf is laid.

Since grass usually grows particularly well in the autumn there is no better time to fill hollows which have developed in established lawns. Faced with a hill and hollow situation the answer is always to fill the hollows rather than to try to lift the turf and cut away soil to reduce the hills.

In the greenhouse

Damping down the house each morning will become less necessary from now on. Since the sun will also be more welcome, shading compounds should be washed off the glass. But ventilation will still be necessary on most days. A little heat at night will help plants like coleus to prosper. Begonias and gloxinias can continue to be watered until their leaves fade. Then the begonias can be left to dry in the soil in a frost free place. Gloxinias should be removed from the pots for drying and storage. Climbers which have finished flowering should be tidied. Plants put out for the summer should be brought in now. Seeds of clarkia, godetia, schizanthus, pansies and violas can all be sown this month. Bedding and rock plant cuttings can be struck now while all cuttings taken last month should be hardened off. Suckers from old shoots and seedlings of calceolarias and cinerarias should be potted on. Stocks sown previously should also be potted up.

Don't forget

To order fruit trees for planting this autumn and winter. When peering at the catalogues it will pay to remember that just about every other fruit tree in the professional orchards is a Cox's Orange Pippin. And while there is no doubt that they are wonderful apples you will be offered them at the greengrocers until well after Christmas. So why not be a bit adventurous and plant something which will be less frequently seen in the shops?

Egremont Russets have a marvellous flavour despite their scurvy skin. Crispin has a munch as satisfying as its name. And the old Orleans Reinnette came very high in the recent eating tests in Paris where they are no mean judges.

If the garden is looking a bit drab now it could provide a better picture next year if you planted September flowering shrubs between now and Christmas. Good candidates are *Abelia x grandiflora* which, given a sunny spot, offers a profusion of pale pink flowers: *Aralia elata* with handsome compound leaves and white flowers; *Callicarpa bodinieri giral-di*, whose rose purple flowers leave dark lilac berries.

Visits

September is the month of the great autumn flower shows where a cornucopia of garden plants and produce is on display. Garden clubs throughout the country ensure that there is plenty to see in each region. Visitors to their shows have the chance of seeing what well-grown crops of new varieties of fruit and vegetables look like and learn about the snags which their growers have encountered.

The autumn displays also include a rich showing of later flowering plants which visitors can consider planting in their own gardens during the dormant season. Shrubs which develop attractive berries in late summer also provide a living catalogue from which subjects can be chosen to enrich our shrubberies.

If possible, efforts should be made to visit the great national autumn shows.

The most notable are the Royal National Rose Society's Autumn Show, at the RHS Hall in London, the National Chrysanthemum Society's Show and the RHS Great Autumn Show at the same venue. The Harrogate Great Autumn Flower Show in the Valley Gardens is also something of a Mecca for northern gardeners.

CREATING CALM CONDITIONS

Autumn is a good time to make major changes in the form of a garden. And one problem for people gardening a fair-sized patch high on a well-drained hillside is providing shelter for plants and people from strong winds.

Calm growing and sitting conditions can be created by a serious effort with a hired motorised digger and driver. This is used to excavate a 'theatre' and place the soil above ground to form high protective banks which can be used to support rocks and make raised beds and as a site to grow trees and shrubs.

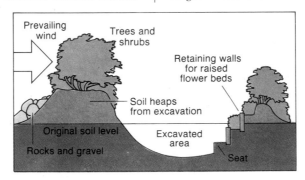

It pays to scrape aside the topsoil from the excavation site for use to top the banks before planting.

When the trees and shrubs are mature the 'below ground' seating area will be well out of the wind.

MULTIPLYING BULBS

Multiplying bulbs like narcissi, hyacinths, nerines and others is so easy that it seems ridiculous not to make the attempt.

The job of actually dividing the bulbs, by a method known as twin-scaling, should not be attempted until the flowers have died back and the bulbs themselves have dried. When you have lifted your chosen specimens, this is what you should do:

1. Swab down work surface with industrial spirit.
2. Remove brown scales and dead roots from a firm and healthy single-nosed bulb.
3. Cut away the dirty outer crust of the basal plate with a sharp surgical scalpel which has been sterilised in a flame.
4. Cut away the top third of the bulb by slicing it cleanly across.
5. Using clean tissue, swab the surface of the bulb with industrial spirit.
6. Place the bulb nose down on the work surface and cut down through it to divide it into wedge-shaped segments with an equal portion of basal plate attached to each segment. A 4in circumference bulb

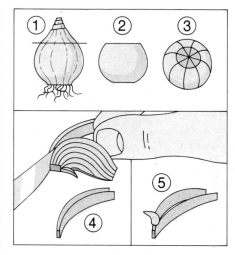

1 Bulb when leaves have died back. 2 Bulb with outer scales removed and nose cut off. 3 Inverted bulb cut into segments. 4 Detaching a pair of scales and a section of basal plate to form the 'twin-scale'. 5 'Twin-scale' with bulbil emerging between scales.

will divide (like a sponge cake) into approximately eight segments.

7. Divide individual segments into twin-scales by peeling back the two outer scales and severing them cleanly from the remainder of the segment by cutting through the basal plate. Repeat until all the twin scales are detached. Place the twin scales into a new 9in by 6in polythene bag as soon as possible to avoid fungal infections.
8. When a maximum of 150 twin scales have been accumulated in a bag add ½ teaspoonful of thiram fungicide and shake thoroughly until all the twin scales are covered with the powder.

9. Add ⅓ pint of horticultural vermiculite which has been moistened with distilled water (by adding 15 volumes of water to 100 volumes of vermiculite).

10. Seal the bag with an elastic band, leaving plenty of room inside for air but ensuring an airtight seal. Shake well to mix the twin scales with the vermiculite.

11. Store the bag in a dark place at a carefully controlled temperature between 60°F and 70°F.

12. In twelve weeks tiny bulbils should have formed on the section of the basal plate between the scales. These should be planted individually 1 inch deep in 3 inch pots containing a 3:1 mixture of sterile peat and sand.

13. Keep the pots in a frost-proof glasshouse.

14. When the leaves have died down in their first summer, refrain from watering. In the autumn, top up the compost and begin watering again.

15. After the leaves have died back in the second summer remove the young bulbs from the pots and store them in a dry place until they are planted out in their final growing place in the garden in the autumn.

16. After another year of fattening in the garden the bulbs should be mature enought to start flowering. Taking natural failures into account, each decent-sized bulb should yield approximately twenty-five flowering bulbs in four years.

PLANTS OF THE MONTH

TREES
Eucryphia x nymanensis 'Nymansay' – white flowers and conspicuous stamens

Sophora japonica – white flowers.

SHRUBS
Aralia elata – huge leaves and white flowers.

Caryopteris x calandonensis – violet blue flowers.

Hydrangea 'Blue Wave' – a purple lacecap.

Dorycrium hirsutum – pinky white flowers.

BORDER PLANTS
Galtonia princeps – deep green flowers.

Gladiolus purpureo-auratus – greenish yellow and purple flowers.

Habranthus flavissima – buttercup yellow flowers.

Leacojum roseum – pale pink flowers.

Liriope muscari – bright violet flowers.

October

If your herbaceous borders are to dazzle your visitors next summer, this month will call for as much resolution and hard work as any other in the year. And if you don't start now you will never finish it in time. So resist all other temptations for the next few weekends and enjoy a few energetic sessions in the garden with your spade and border fork.

Ground work

Mark out the boundaries of any new borders you plan to establish, then remove the turf and double-dig the whole area, incorporating plenty of manure as you go. Leave the top surface rough, to be broken down by winter weather.

A very good way of ensuring that new beds have smoothly curved edges is to lay hosepipe on the ground and push it about until it forms the curve you require. The pipe can then be used as a line against which to place the back of the spade blade when cutting into the ground. A long board laid on the ground makes a good edge when straight lines are required.

Many of the herbaceous plants in your established borders will need lifting every three years if they are to remain robust and prosper. So examine each plant closely and if it is becoming thin in the crown and straggly or excessively woody, remove it completely from the bed, using a spade and a crowbar if necessary. And, if you want to ensure their survival, lift dahlia tubers and gladioli corms now for storing indoors.

When everything that needs to come out has been lifted, there will be large clear areas of the bed which should now be dug over thoroughly. Really rotted and well-broken-up manure can be added and mixed into the soil with a fork at this stage.

Any areas of the vegetable plot which are free can also be dug over and left rough this month. If they haven't been double-dug and well fed for a few years they will crop better next year if this technique is employed now.

If you plan to plant fruit trees later it's a good idea to prepare the planting holes now. Gravel paths should be rolled and repaired where necessary.

This is also a good time to make any major alterations, such as the creation of new paths and steps, building walls (before severe frost becomes a problem and affects the setting of cement) or substantially changing the contours of your garden by moving large quantities of earth.

Pruning

You will obtain a clearer impression of which herbaceous plants need lifting and dividing when cutting them back after the majority of them have finished flowering. Cut back asparagus foliage. Cut away old wood from figs to allow plenty of room for new growth. Loganberry and autumn-fruiting raspberry canes should be cut down to ground level.

Cleaning and tidying

Sweep leaves and other plant trash from lawns, paths and the foot of hedges. Don't add it to the compost because tree leaves and twiggy materials rot too slowly. Make a separate heap by mixing it with some soil.

Outdoor planting

After dividing plants lifted from the herbaceous border, select healthy sections of root with strong young shoots attached and plant them suitably spaced in groups of three or five. Next year these will develop into the bold clumps which can add real majesty to a border. If enough plants of a single type are available try to arrange them in thick drifts which flow behind and in front of similar drifts of other types.

Make the main planting of tulips this month – look for bulbs of the older, less vulgar species. It is also a good time to plant anemones and winter aconite. And don't delay finishing all your other 'spring' bulb planting.

While planting, don't forget to place a few narcissi in bulb fibre in a bowl and just bury it beneath the soil in the garden. Leave it there until the shoots have become 2in long before lifting the bowl and keeping it in a warm light place in the house. They could well be in flower by Christmas. Lift China asters which have grown on well since flowering and put them in pots to take indoors where they will flower again later in the year.

Plant out seedling pansies, biennial and perennial seedlings and hardy spring-flowering plants of all descriptions. Cabbages, endive and lettuce can be transplanted to a warm corner of the vegetable patch or to a cold frame. Plant new rhubarb crowns and globe artichokes. It is a good idea to plant Jerusalem artichoke tubers in a line so they will form a pretty hedge to screen the other vegetables from the wind. Their large daisies also make useful cut flowers in the summer.

Planting of new fruit trees or soft fruit canes can be carried out if you can obtain deliveries. If you want to move trees and shrubs, now is one of the best times to do it, particularly the evergreens. Try to move them with as large a rootball of soil as possible and water them frequently in the first three months after transplanting.

Crocus speciosus seem so impatient to display their charming deeply veined cups that the flowers often appear before their leaves. Their presence in sizeable groups makes the onset of autumn seem less gloomy.

Visits

Before the worst of the wintery weather arrives to halt serious ground work sensible gardeners choose October as the month when they make the most ambitious changes to their gardens. And before doing major excavation to establish terraces, flights of steps, new ponds, paths, beds etc. it is wise to discover what can be achieved at home by visiting as many gardens as possible which include similar features. Often it is only little, but none the less vital, ideas which can be picked up on these visits, such as ways of providing the firm edgings that paving slabs laid on sand need if they are not to drift.

Aware of your likely building and gross landscaping activities, garden centre managers always ensure that they display and stock their widest range of masonry items in October. Since there is plenty of competition, visit as many of them as you can to obtain a real picture of what is available and which centres offer the best prices.

Outdoor sowing

Continue sowing sweet peas over enriched trenches. Early peas can also be sown in a protected area of the vegetable garden. Sow some corn salad to provide colour and vitamins in the winter. Radishes and spinach may still be sown.

Lawn work

Examine the lawn carefully to locate low points. After a thorough spiking to reduce compaction, treat it with an insecticide to control leatherjackets, which can do great damage in the autumn, and then fill the hollows with a mixture of sieved loam and sharp sand. Broadcast an autumn lawn fertiliser which is high in phosphates to stimulate good root growth.

In the greenhouse

Pick the remaining fruit from tomato vines and then sterilise the soil they have grown in or empty out and sterilise their pots or rings. Scatter the residual compost from grow-bags on the compost heap or on the borders. Pot up strong young hollyhock seedlings from the garden and bring them in to the glasshouse for the winter.

Avoid over-ventilating the greenhouse from now on and ensure that any thermostatically controlled heating systems are working properly. Arum lilies should be repotted. Water pelargoniums sparingly, taking care not to wet the leaves.

Nip out the tops of sweet peas, clarkia and schizanthus seedlings. Take any cuttings you need of shrubby calceolarias, periwinkles, phloxes, salvias, verbenas, etc. and bring pot roses inside.

Cauliflower seedlings should be pricked out and stood in frames. Lift two-year-old rhubarb crowns now and leave them packed in boxes in a warm, dark corner to force their shoots.

Don't forget

To lift remaining root vegetables and store them in damp peat or sand; to thin out any lettuces sown under cloches last month; to pick any remaining apples and pears and store them in a cool, well-ventilated place.

If you have a dessert grape-vine which has done particularly well, remove bunches of grapes from it and dip their cut stalks in hot candle wax to seal them. Then hang them upside down in a cool, well-ventilated, dark place suspended from string wound through the main stalks. Stored this way, each grape will hang away from its neighbour, rot will be reduced to a minimum and you will be eating your own fresh grapes right through until the end of January. Inspect them once a fortnight and cut away any which are spoiling.

A HARLEQUIN PATH

If you find your garden paths boring and would like to give them a more decorative allure a cheerier topping is easy to make. Wooden batten (1½in wide) is used to make a pattern on the ground between well-set brick path edging (see illustration). This will serve to separate contrasting aggregates (such as white

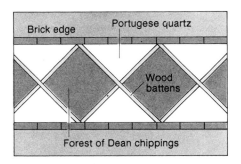

crushed Portuguese quartz and pink Forest of Dean rock) to form a simple harlequin design. The same technique can be used to produce more ambitious patterns if you have the patience to work out and make the batten separations.

A CIRCULAR BED

A century ago, in the days before radio and television, 25,000 people regularly visited Battersea Park on summer Sunday evenings to view spectacular 'carpet beds'. These highly formalised plant treats were loved by the Victorians. But it must be admitted that on a grand scale they demanded a lot of planning and labour. However, gardeners with facilities to raise annuals from seed and sufficient

spare time available might like to reproduce on a small scale one of the designs which made people gasp in the summer of 1878.

A circular bed should be planted according to the plan shown in the illustration. It has a margin (1) of *Sedum acre elegans*, a band (2) of *Calocephalus brownii* and an inner line (3) carried round the rays of the star and circle of *Alternanthera amoena*, the rays and centre (4) being planted with *Sedum glaucum* dotted with *Pachyphyton bracteosum*, and the angles (5) with the same sedum dotted with *Cacalia tomentosa*.

Plants of the Month

Trees
Malus 'Golden Hornet' – bright yellow crab apples.
Cotoneaster frigidus 'Notcutts var.' – crimson berries

Shrubs
Fatsia japonica – white flower globes.
Osmanthus heterophyllus – perfumed white flowers.
Vinca minor 'Bowles var.' – blue flowers.
Daboecia cantabrica Atropurpurea – purple flowers.

Border Plants
Tricyrtis hirta alba – white flowers.
Schizostylus coccinea – crimson flowers.
Cyclamen mirabile – pink flowers.
Allium callimischon – pink lined white flowers.
Kniphofia galpinii – orange flowers.

November

Before the land becomes too sodden, as much as possible of the recontouring and major digging must be accomplished this month. Otherwise it may not be possible to work the soil until the spring when many other jobs will press for priority attention.

Ground work

Don't fail to hoe out weeds before they become established between the vegetables. This is also a good time to carry out major drainage works – a task which has become much easier since the introduction of the new thin-section plastic drainage conduit. The benefit will be land fit to work earlier next spring. Spread as much manure as possible round the plants in the herbaceous border and scuffle it into the topsoil with a fork.

Pruning

As soon as the leaves have fallen, apple and pear trees should be given their major pruning. Consult a good fruit manual (*The Fruit Garden Displayed*, published by the Royal Horticultural Society, offers useful advice) if you are doubtful about which twigs and branches to remove.

Complete pruning of cultivated blackberries. Use the secateurs very carefully to form pyramid, cordon or espaliered fruit trees. Prune roses, but don't cut them too short now.

Security

Weed strawberries carefully to prevent insidious competition. Spray apple and pear trees to control canker if it is seen to be developing. Two sprays of copper fungicide are necessary: the first just before leaf fall and the second when 50 per cent of the leaf has fallen. This is also the time to apply the same spray to control leaf curl on peaches and apricots. Apply dalapon to suppress weeds round established apples, pears, blackcurrants, gooseberries and cane fruit. Paint on insecticide to control woolly aphid colonies, noticed as white patches in cracks in fruit-tree bark. Aphids and caterpillars can still do bad damage to vegetables at this time of the year so watch out for them and spray with a permethrin-based insecticide if necessary. Slugs, too, begin to threaten again under damp autumn conditions. Clear up insect and fungal attacks on roses before the winter by giving them a thorough soaking with a combined insecticidal and fungicidal spray. After cutting back the old flower shoots, spray the crowns of Michaelmas daisies with a fungicide to control mildew.

Spray cleared areas with complete weedkiller to control couch and other grasses. Be sure that the effect of the weedkiller you choose will not be too persistent and thwart your next spring's planting plans. Control moss and worms in lawns by applying the appropriate dressing.

Fumigate the greenhouse with an anti-pest-and-disease smoke to prevent insects and plant pathogens lurking there through the winter.

Icy winds and low temperature are inevitable over the next few months. Evergreens, while capable of surviving, can be severely scorched and take a long time to recover. Tender wall shrubs will not survive unless they are given protection. Evergreens on windy corners can be shrouded in fine netting or, less beautiful, polythene sheeting. Polythene on wooden frames can be leaned over wall shrubs and the gaps at the end can be blocked with cut evergreen boughs or sacking. Straw or bracken provide a good protection for the crowns of tender herbaceous plants or small shrubs.

Tall brassicas and other tall and delicate plants can be supported by attaching them to canes. Heel round established and newly planted rose bushes to reduce windrock. Turn over leaves to protect the curds of late cauliflowers and early broccoli.

Outdoor planting

This is the ideal time to complete the planting of all bare root ornamental trees or bushes. Anemones, canterbury bells, pansies, primroses, sweet williams, violets and wallflowers can still be planted out. It is also a good time to plant iris tubers. Settle them with the top surface just exposed, on to a low mound of coarse grit, which will prevent them from becoming waterlogged. Tulips may still be planted. Continue to plant cabbage, savoys and leeks in the vegetable garden.

Outdoor sowing

Sow broad beans and peas in the vegetable plot.

Feeding

Dress asparagus beds with a thick layer of manure. This should also be spread between the strawberry rows. Spread lime on land which carried brassicas this year, or in any patches of high acidity.

Lawn work

Keep the lawn clear of fallen leaves and debris. Tidy and repair lawn edges. If they can't be tidied by cutting their edges with a sharp spade, remove the rough turf and replace with new. When cutting away a damaged area, don't be finicky – take off a decent-sized rectangle and replace it. Mowing with the blades set high

Cyclamen neapolitanum (hederifolium) – thought
by many gardeners to be the most exquisite of
the small cyclamens, they luxuriate in a thick
covering of leaf mould in a shady corner and will
thrive in rather dry places.

will keep the lawn looking tidy if growth has continued, it will also help to chop up fallen leaves.

Maintenance

If you grow soft fruit and vegetables in a cage, ensure that all the wire mesh is in good order and well attached to its frame. Make sure, too, that the 'bird-proof' door really fits and remove the 'roof' netting to avoid it becoming a snow-collector which could bring the whole structure down in a blizzard. This is a good time to have vital equipment like lawn mowers and cultivators serviced. Since most people keep putting off this task, you should receive excellent service at this time of year. Afterwards, store the machines in a well-ventilated, dry place.

In the greenhouse

If your greenhouse is old, make sure that its door and ventilators can be well sealed to keep out chilling draughts which could ruin your plants in really cold weather. Test any thermostatically-controlled heating equipment. Use a thermometer and take some time to make sure that it is functioning correctly. If it is slow to cut off when the desired setting temperature is reached, the malfunction could cost you a lot of money. Failure to function when the temperature plunges could lead to a disastrous loss of plants.

This is the time to stop feeding most greenhouse plants and cut back on water-ing. Considerable heat saving can be achieved by lining the greenhouse with the kind of polythene sheeting that has air bubbles in it. You will have to decide what temperature you wish to maintain in the greenhouse and be sure that your heating system is adequate to meet the challenge of sub-zero nights. In order to save money, most people opt for a temperature of 4°C to 7°C (40°F to 45°F). This will allow many plants over-wintering in the greenhouse to survive. But anything of sub-tropical origin will have to be taken to a bright place inside the house.

Many gardeners find it useful to create mini-hothouses on their greenhouse benches. Cable heaters sunk in a gravel base will allow quite high temperatures to be maintained inside a 'tent' created by fixing polythene sheeting over a light wooden frame. Such mini-hothouses can be used as a winter home for some of the more tender species (see 'January').

Prick out and pot on late seedlings. Remove dead leaves from calceolarias and cinerarias and when necessary shift them into larger pots. Put pansies in the warmest part of the greenhouse. Sow cyclamen seed for next year's plants. Dig out and pot up azaleas and deutzias and bring them into the greenhouse to be forced into early bloom.

Plant bulbs in pots for early flowering. Sink the pots in soil outside and cover them with peat to encourage rooting. When the first shoots begin to show they can be brought into the greenhouse for forcing. Prepare for early spring planting-out in the vegetable patch by sowing dwarf beans and lettuce in boxes in the greenhouse now.

Don't forget

To select and order supplies of early potato seed for next year. Be sure to ventilate the greenhouse well on warm, sunny days.

Visits

This is the month when some of the most extraordinary autumn colours can be seen in British gardens. They can be sampled at their best in great gardens where large areas have been established as woodland or shrubbery. These are places where trees like maples, liquidamber, nyssas and stewartia or shrubs like enkianthus, eucryphia glutinosa, hamamelis or clethras have been planted deliberately for their autumn effects. But even commonplaces like hawthorns can enchant as their leaves become stained scarlet or fade to a buttercup yellow.

Some fine parks in which to view the autumn spectacular are Killerton, near Exeter, Devon; Sheffield Park, near Uckfield, East Sussex; Rievaulx, near Helmsley, North Yorkshire; the Valley Gardens, Windsor Great Park; Waddesdon Manor, near Aylesbury, Buckinghamshire; Tatton Park, near Knutsford, Cheshire; Wallington Hall, near Belsay, Northumberland; Scone Palace, near Perth in Scotland.

GARBAGE BIN LILY POND

Gardeners often complain that although they would enjoy a little water feature in their garden they don't feel like making the effort of excavating a real pond.

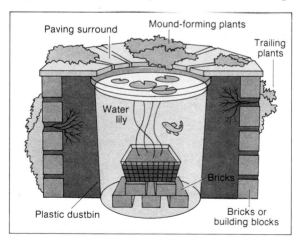

Paving surround — Mound-forming plants — Trailing plants — Water lily — Bricks — Plastic dustbin — Bricks or building blocks

They and other gardeners who for some reason or another cannot excavate concreted yards can however have a mini lily pond for a minimum of work at little cost.

The key to the whole operation is the purchase of a large plastic moulded garbage bin. Once sited in an attractive location this can be surrounded by a circular wall of bricks or building blocks (see diagram). If earth is used to fill the gap between the wall and the bin trailing plants can be grown in gaps deliberately left in the wall to take them.

Paving slabs laid on top of the wall and overhanging the rim of the bin will disguise its plastic nature. Mound-forming plants can be grown in cracks between the slabs. When the bin is filled with water it will be deep enough to allow a waterlily to be grown in a basket of compost set below the surface, on a pile of bricks. The gaps between these bricks will act as splendid hidey holes for fish.

SAFE CLIPPING

One of the trickiest and most dangerous jobs in a garden is clipping a tall hedge of immature trees. The problem is that the main stems of the trees are not strong enough to support the man on the ladder needed to clip their top areas of canopy.

A simple and effective answer is to firmly rope a long (8ft) stout board across the top of the ladder. When the board is laid across the high sections of the trees the weight of the ladder and anyone on it

will be supported by several main stems (see diagram) and clipping can be carried out in safety.

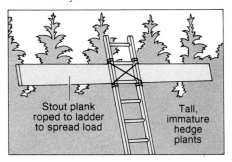

Stout plank roped to ladder to spread load

Tall, immature hedge plants

PLANTS OF THE MONTH

TREES
Prunus subhirtella autumnalis – pink flowers.

Malus 'Evereste' – red striped yellow crab apples.

SHRUBS
Viburnum farreri – scented white flowers.

Lonicera standishii – cream flowers with sweet scent.

Mahonia acanthifolia – yellow flowers.

Eleagnus pungens maculata – bright gold-splashed leaves and small silvery, scented flowers.

BORDER PLANTS
Cyclamen cilicium – shell pink flowers

Galanthus corcyrenis – an early flowering snowdrop

Iris unguicularis 'Mary Barnard' – deep purple and gold flowers.

Erica praecox rubra – deep red flowers.

Erica vulgaris 'H.E.Beale' – pink flowers.

December

December is always considered by old hands to be the month of the catalogue, pencil and graph paper. Unless the weather is unusually mild and the land very dry, activities outdoors are limited. So there are other priorities, like planning next year's cropping in the vegetable plot or ordering new plants to fit a redrawn general layout of the garden. Graph paper is very useful for planning; make the large squares represent a square foot and you can more easily assess the actual number of plants required. If the weather is fine there are still plenty of enjoyable outdoor jobs.

Ground work

When the soil isn't too wet get on with the digging. The sooner that's finished the better. Then the rough topsoil will be exposed to the beneficial effects of wind, rain, freezing and thawing to crumble it finely for next spring's planting. Press carnations, pinks, pansies, roses etc. firmly into the ground after severe frosts, which tend to lift and loosen them.

Continue hoeing the ground between growing crops in the vegetable garden.

Security

As fruit trees and bushes lose their final leaves and become dormant start spraying them with a tar-oil winter wash to control aphids, suckers and scale insects. Begin with stone fruits like plums and greengages. Inspect fruit in storage and remove anything which is rotting. Spray established strawberry beds with simazine to control weeds. Check all stakes and ties on newly planted trees and shrubs to ensure that they are sound. Inspect apple and pear trees for canker and apply a treatment where necessary. Continue to bait for slugs where any foliage damage is observed. When winter-washing fruit don't ignore ornamentals like prunus and malus species, chaenomeles, cotoneaster and flowering currant. Treat paths and steps with moss and algae killer to prevent slippery surfaces developing. Whenever it snows shake fresh fall out of evergreen trees immediately, otherwise the weight of accumulated snow could cause serious damage.

Remember that mice love stored fruit, vegetables, flower corms and bulbs so keep them in a safe place and bait for the mice. Place cloches over as many of the young plants in the vegetable plot as possible.

Cleaning and tidying

Take a broom, shovel and bucket round paved areas, not forgetting their hidden corners and sweep up the last of the autumn leaf debris. In well-trodden places it can become very slimy and dangerous and presents an obvious danger on dark evenings and at party time. If it is allowed to accumulate and rot on top of plants some of them will be ruined. If the weather is too chilly for outdoor work tidy up the greenhouse so that everything is ready for the rush of spring activity.

Outdoor planting

This is the best month for planting climbers. But only do it on a day when overnight frost seems unlikely. If they arrive in hard weather loosen their packing and keep them in a frost-free place until conditions improve. It is still possible to plant rose trees on milder days. All bareroot fruit trees can also be planted this month. When the forecast is for a prolonged cold spell it is better to loosen the bundles and heel the plants into a shallow trench of just-moist soil and leave them until conditions improve.

Outdoor sowing

In milder areas further sowings of broad beans and round peas can be made to obtain early crops next year. Make sure that the seed is treated to protect it

Prunus subhirtella – the rosebud cherry is perhaps the best and least widely grown of these flowering trees. It has the wonderful advantage of flowering over a long period and if one show of blossom is damaged by heavy frost it rapidly produces another.

against pests and diseases. Seeds of shrubs like berberis, cotoneaster and pieris can be sown in an outdoor bed where the cold weather will encourage germination. Camellia and magnolia seed should also be sown now.

Lawn work

After heavy rain, when the water table is high and the ditches and brooks are gorg-ed, examine the lawn carefully to identify the really wet areas. Note them so that the drainage can be improved next season. If a mild spell has encouraged the grass to grow and become too lanky give the lawn its final topping of the year with the cutter blade set high. On heavy soil the less traffic on a lawn at this time of year the better. And if you have to wheel loaded barrows across it do make a pathway of planks.

In the greenhouse

Continue to be sparing with the water and take care to open the vents on sunny days. Keep cactus bone dry this month to avoid rotting. Potted azaleas, deutzias, similar shrubs and lilies can be placed in the warmer corners and begin to be forced. Freesias, small hyacinths and narcissi can be very gently forced. Lilies of the valley from outside can be potted up and urged on with a little heat. If there are any signs of green or white fly the greenhouse should be fumigated with an insecticidal smoke generator.

Strawberry plants potted up and standing outside can be brought into the greenhouse so that they will provide an early crop next year. Continue to pot on cinerarias, primulas and annuals before they become pot-bound. Lettuces can now be planted in the ground as well as plants of fig, peach, nectarine or grape.

Remember that these fruit trees will occupy a lot of space and could rob other greenhouse plants of essential light. Plant them on the north side with the intention of training them up that wall of the house then gradually allowing them to grow at roof level towards the south.

Pruning

Try to finish the fruit trees soon, but resist the temptation to use secateurs when heavy frost is expected. Collect and burn all the prunings to avoid spreading disease. Mulch with straw or bracken those areas where hardwood cuttings of shrubs and trees are being rooted in open ground.

Visits

With all the rush and frivolity preceding Christmas there isn't much time or much reason to indulge in conventional garden visiting. However, gardeners with gardening friends or relations can spend useful hours gift hunting at the garden centres which have proliferated on the fringes of most of our towns of recent years.

A large number of people with small lawns still rely upon an ancient manual machine to do their lawn mowing. This is a needless burden when quite a small investment could these days change their lives by providing a small mains electric machine. Some of the electric mowers on offer can be guided by a single handle which makes them a boon to gardeners who for one reason or another need to use a walking stick.

When buying gifts for other gardeners do be practical – look for gloves too tough to be shredded quickly by eager dogs or hand forks with handles and prongs strong enough to withstand some levering when caught by hidden boulders.

And if you can't think of a gift for the already well-equipped gardener why not send a donation in his/her name to the Gardens for the Disabled Trust (Hon. Sec. Mrs. Susan van Laun, Old House

Farm, Peasmarsh, Near Rye, East Sussex, TN31 6YD) which is a registered charity which provides practical and financial assistance to help disabled people wishing to take an active part in gardening.

ON TOP OF THE ARCHES

Really strong trellising is hard to find and very expensive. And it is surprising to discover how few gardeners make their own, even though the least gifted DIYers can usually produce something very satisfactory.

After all it doesn't require much talent to drill holes at regular intervals in 1in square section timber and then screw it to other lengths of the same material to form the traditional rectangular or diamond patterns. It is, however, worth ensuring that the screws are cadmium-plated to resist corrosion because this will ensure that the trellis lasts much longer.

What has always proved more difficult for amateurs is the provision of satisfactory arches. An easy way to accomplish

this (see illustration) is to use easy-to-bend builder's lathes. When coated with contact adhesive they can be formed round a semi-circular line of nails hammered into a board.

Each end of the lathe can be held firmly in place with a mole wrench which can be undone and closed again to allow the insertion of each new strip of lathe. Five strips will make up an arch roughly 1in by 1in in section.

SAFE STEPS

Stout logs held in place by steel pickets make pleasing rustic steps up woody banks in gardens. Their main handicap is the fact that they can become dangerously slippery in wet weather – particularly in the autumn when covered with leaves.

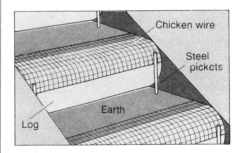

A simple way to overcome this problem is to cover the log treads with a layer of chicken wire attached to the surface with 'U' nails (see illustration).

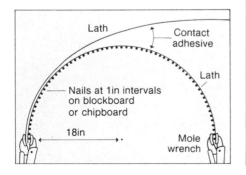

PLANTS OF THE MONTH

TREES

Ilex aquifolium 'J.C. van Tol' – dark shining leaves and red fruit.

Salix alba chermesina – bright orange scarlet young twigs.

SHRUBS

Hamamelis mollis – yellow flowers.

Jasminium nudiflorum – yellow flowers.

Lonicera fragrantissima – scented cream flowers.

Mahonia x media – yellow flowers.

BORDER PLANTS

Erica carnea 'Springwood White' – white flowers.

Lamiastrum galeobdolon variegatum – silver-flushed, heart-shaped leaves.

Petasites fragrans – honey-scented pink flowers.

Cyclamen coum – pink to crimson flowers.

Helichrysum splendidum – bright silver foliage.

Metric Conversion Table

(approximate figures)

1 inch = 2.54 cm
1 foot = 30.48 cm
1 yard = 91.44 cm
1 acre = 0.405 ha
1 cubic foot = $0.03m^3$
1 cubic yard = $0.07m^3$
1 ounce = 28.35 g
1 pound = 0.454 kg
1 hundredweight = 50.80 kg

1 centimetre = 0.394 in
1 metre = 39.37 in
1 hectare = 2.471 acres
1 cubic metre = $1.31 yd^3$
1 kilogram = 2.205 lb

millimetre = mm
centimetre = cm
metre = m
cubic metre = m^3
hectare = ha
kilogram = kg

Index

cactus, 118
calceolaria, 14, 35, 74, 83, 92, 102, 110
calendula, 33
Callicarpa bodinieri giraldi, 86
Calocephalus brownii, 104
camellias, 35, 65, 117
Camellia susanqua, 17
Camellia x williamsii 'Bow Bells', 47
campanula, 33, 66
Campanula carpatica, 57
Campsis radicans, 22
cannas, 64
Canterbury bells, 64, 108
carnations, 32, 44, 64, 115
carrots, 14, 24, 33, 51, 64
Caryopteris x calandonensis, 95
cauliflower, 24, 33, 52, 82, 102, 108
ceanothus, 65
Ceanothus arboreus 'Trewithen Blue', 57
celery, 52, 72, 81, 82
celosia, 35
chaenomeles, 115
Chamaecyparis lawsoniana-elwoodii, 76
cherries, 62, 71, 89; Morello, 51
chervil, 33, 52
Chiastophyllum oppositifolium, 57
Chimonanthus praecox, 27
chives, 32, 33
chrysanthemums, 14, 24, 32, 71
Chrysanthemum maximum 'Wirral
Supreme', 85
cineraria, 74, 83, 92, 110, 118
cistus, 65, 76
clarkia, 32, 92, 102
clematis, 22
Clematis cirrhosa, 13, 17
clethras, 111
climbing plants, 26, 41, 62-4, 74, 82,
    89, 116; supporting, 84-5
Clitoria 'Double Blue Sails', 54
cloches, 16, 24; building a Super-cloche,
    35-6, *36*
colchicum, 82
coleus, 92
compost 11, 12, 21, 24-5, 31, 44, 61, 81,
    89; making a perfect heap, 36-7, *37*; in
    planted walls, 56

conifers, cuttings from, 76, *76*
coral tree, 54-5
coreopsis, 32
Coreopsis verticillata Grandiflora, 86
corn salad, 34, 82, 102
Cornus florida 'White Cloud', 57
Cornus macrophylla, 78
Cornus mas, 27
Coronilla valentina glauca, 23, 27
cosmos, 32
cotoneaster 115, 117; cuttings from, 76
Cotoneaster frigidus 'Notcutts var.', 104
courgettes, 36, 42, 64
Cox's Orange Pippin, 92
Crispin apple, 92
Crocosmia 'Emberglow', 78
crocus, 90
Crocus aureus, 27
Crocus speciosus, 101
cucumber, 25, 45, 64
Cupressocyparis leylandii, 76
cyclamen, 74, 82, 83, 110
Cyclamen balearicum, 27
Cyclamen cilicium, 112
Cyclamen coum, 17, 120
Cyclamen mirabile, 104
Cyclamen neapolitanum (hederifolium),
    109
Cyclamen persicum, 27
cytisus, cuttings from, 76

Daboecia cantabrica Atropurpurea, 104
daisies, 52
dahlias, 14, 34, 44, 72, 89, 90, 91
Daphne mezereum, 27
delphiniums, 22, 51
deutzia, cuttings from, 76, 110, 118
Dianthus arvernensis, 57
Dicentra eximea 'Adrian Bloom', 86
Dierama pumila, 86
digging, 11, 16, 21, 31, 41, 45-6, 51, 81,
    89, 99, 107, 115
dill, 33
Dorycrium hirsutum, 95

Egremont Russets, 92
eleagnus, 65

Indigofera gerardiana, 79
iris, 64, 72, 90, 108
Iris unguicularis, 17
Iris unguicularis 'Lazica', 38
Iris unguicularis 'Mary Barnard', 112
Iris unguicularis 'Mary McIlroy', 57
Itea ilicifolia, 86

Juniperus tamariskifolia, 76
jasmine, 22
Jasminium nudiflorum, 120

kale, 34, 52, 72
Kniphofia galpinii, 104
Keolreuteria paniculata, 86

Laburnum alpinum, 68
Lamiastrum galeobdolon Variegatum, 120
larkspur, 32
lavatera, 33
lavender, 41; hedges, 81
lawns, 11, 13, 21, 24, 34, 44, 54, 64, 71,
    72, 90-92, 102, 108-9, 117; aerating,
    14, 54, 102; feeding, 34, 64, 102;
    'instant', 92; levelling, 92, 102;
    mowing, 13-14, 44, 64, 72, 90,
    108-9, 117
leeks, 14, 24, 35, 44, 52, 61, 64, 81, 108
Leptospermum scorparium 'Red Damask',
    68
lettuces, 13, 16, 24, 34, 44, 72, 82, 90,
    100, 102, 111, 118; in mini-hothouse,
    15
Leucojum roseum, 95
Liatris callilepsis, 85
Ligustrum lucidum 'Latifolium', 86
lilacs, 12, 62
lilies, 12, 14, 82-3, 90, 118
Lilium 'Green Dragon', 78
Lilium pumilum, 68
Lilium tigrinum splendens, 86
lily of the valley, 118
liquidamber, 111
Liriodendron tulipfera aureo marginatum,
    68
Liriope muscari, 95
lobelia, 24, 44

loganberries, 11, 31, 52, 81, 100
Lonicera fragrantissima, 17
Lonicera standishii, 112
lupins, 33

magnolia, 117
Magnolia campbellii, 27
Magnolia grandiflora, 41
Magnolia stellata, 47
Mahonia acanthifolia, 112
Mahonia 'Charity', 17
Mahonia x media, 120
malus, 115
Malus 'Golden Hornet', 104
Malus 'Evereste', 112
maples, 111
marguerites, 35
marjoram, 33, 42
marrows, 25, 35, 45
melon, 25, 35, 45
Mentha requienii, 57
Michaelmas daisies, 22, 108
Mignonette 'Fragrant Beauty', 83
mini-hothouse, making, *15*
mint, 32
Monarda 'Cambridge Scarlet', 85
montbretia, 44, 90
mountain fescue grass, 66

narcissus, 82, 90, 94; forcing, 100, 118
Narcissus bulbocodium, 33
Narcissus cyclamineus, 38
nasturtium, 33
nectarines, 13, 22, 51, 81, 118
nemesia, 35
nerines, 94
nicotiana, 35
nigella, 33
nyssas, 111

olearia, 41
Olearia x scilloniensis, 57
onions, 14, 21, 24, 34, 42, 44, 52, 64, 82,
    89
Orleans Reinnette, 92
Osmanthus x burkwoodii, 47
Osmanthus heterophyllus, 104